Kant

on Happiness in Ethics

SUNY Series in Ethical Theory
Robert B. Louden, Editor

Kant

on Happiness in Ethics

Victoria S. Wike

State University of New York Press

Published by
State University of New York Press, Albany

Printed in the United States of America

For information, address State University of New York Press, State University Plaza, Albany, N.Y. 12246

Production by E. Moore
Marketing by Bernadette LaManna

Library of Congress Cataloging-in-Publication Data

Wike, Victoria S.
Kant on happiness in ethics / Victoria S. Wike.
p. cm. — (SUNY series in ethical theory)
Includes bibliographical references and index.
ISBN 0-7914-1973-8 (HC : alk. paper). — ISBN 0-7914-1974-6 (PB : alk. paper)
1. Kant, Immanuel, 1724-1804—Ethics. 2. Happiness. I. Title. II. Series.
B2799.H36W55 1994
170—dc20 93-23225
CIP

10 9 8 7 6 5 4 3 2 1

Contents

Abbreviations

All references to Kant's work are in the text. I have put first the page number of the English translation, followed by the volume number and the page number of the German text. References to the German text are to the Royal Prussian Academy edition of *Kants Gesammelte Schriften.* The one exception is Paul Menzer's edition of *Eine Vorlesung Kant's über Ethik* (Berlin: Pan Verlag Rolf Heise, 1924). References to this German text list M, followed by the page number from the text.

The abbreviations for the English translations are these:

- A/B First and second editions of the *Critique of Pure Reason*, trans. Norman Kemp Smith (New York: St. Martin's, 1965).
- CJ *Critique of Judgment*, trans. J. H. Bernard (New York: Hafner, 1951).
- CPR *Critique of Practical Reason*, trans. Lewis White Beck (Indianapolis: Bobbs-Merrill, 1956).
- Gr. *Groundwork of the Metaphysic of Morals*, trans. H. J. Paton (New York: Harper, 1964).
- LE *Lectures on Ethics*, trans. Louis Infield (New York: Harper & Row, 1963).
- MM "The Metaphysical Principles of Virtue" (often called the *Tugendlehre*; part 2 of the *Metaphysics of Morals*), trans. James Ellington (New York: Bobbs-Merrill, 1964).
- Rel. *Religion Within the Limits of Reason Alone*, trans. Theodore M. Greene and Hoyt H. Hudson (New York: Harper, 1960).
- TP *On the Old Saw: That May Be Right in Theory But It Won't Work in Practice*, trans. E. B. Ashton (Philadelphia: University of Pennsylvania Press, 1974).

Preface

Kant's ethics is taught in practically every introductory ethics class although it is notoriously hard in such a context to do Kant justice. The result is that Kant's treatment of ethics is simplified and caricatured. Kant is often taken to advocate an ethic precisely opposite in orientation to those propounded by Aristotle and Mill. It is said that while they are consequentialists, interested in the ends of ethics, Kant is a nonconsequentialist, not interested in the ends of ethics. Kant's ethics, it is claimed, focuses only on duty, on principles, and not on the objects or ends of moral agents.

My aim is to contribute to the combating of this simplistic view of Kant's ethics. There are several ways this simplistic view can be overcome. One way is to focus on Kant's concern for objective ends, for persons as ends in themselves, and for the ultimate end, the highest good. Ends play an important role in Kant's ethic in spite of his nonconsequentialism. I show this in the discussions of ends as determining grounds and the highest good. Another way is to consider Kant's treatment of happiness, that end of special importance to consequentialists like Aristotle and Mill. By examining Kant's account of happiness in ethics, I show that while Kant is opposed to happiness as a principle of ethics, he does value happiness (as a natural end), and his ethics is concerned with the pursuit of happiness (as a means to morality and as a part of the highest good). This study considers the meaning and role of happiness and of ends in Kant's ethics in order to provide a more complete and accurate view of his ethics.

I would like to thank Loyola University Chicago for twice providing me with leave time to write this work.

Also, thanks is due to those graduate students who helped with library searches and discussed Kant and happiness in class with me. Finally, I want to thank Rachel, John, and Molly who have taught me a lot about happiness.

Acknowledgments

I wish to thank the following publishers for granting permission for use of materials from the following:

Quotations from *Critique of Practical Reason* by Immanuel Kant and translated by Lewis White Beck are reprinted with the permission of Macmillan College Publishing Company. Copyright © 1956 by Macmillan College Publishing Company, Inc.

Quotations from *Groundwork of the Metaphysic of Morals* by Immanuel Kant and translated by H. J. Paton are reprinted with the permission of Random Century Group Ltd. Copyright © 1964 by Hutchinson Publishing.

Quotations from *Lectures on Ethics* by Immanuel Kant and translated by Louis Infield are reprinted with the permission of Methuen and Company, Publishers. Copyright © 1963 by Harper & Row, Publishers, Inc.

Quotations from "The Metaphysical Principles of Virtue" (Part 2 of the *Metaphysics of Morals*) by Immanuel Kant and translated by James Ellington are reprinted with the permission of Hackett Publishing Company, Inc. Copyright © 1964 by Hackett Publishing Company, Inc.; all rights reserved.

Quotations from *Religion within the Limits of Reason Alone* by Immanuel Kant and translated by Theodore M. Greene & Hoyt H. Hudson are reprinted with the permission of Open Court Publishing Company. Copyright © 1960 by Open Court Publishing Company.

I am also grateful to the editors and publishers who allowed me to use material from my articles: "Kant on Happiness," *Philosophy Research Archives* 13 (1987-88) 79-90 (used with permission of the Philosophy Documentation Center, publisher of *Philosophy Research Archives*); "The Role of Happiness in Kant's *Groundwork*,"

The Journal of Value Inquiry 21 (1987) 73-79 and "Does Kant's ethics require that the moral law be the sole determining ground of the will?," *The Journal of Value Inquiry* 27 (1993) 85-92 (both reprinted by permission of Kluwer Academic Publishers); and "Kant on the Indirect Duty to Pursue Happiness," *Akten des 7. Internationalen Kant-Kongresses* (Bonn: Bouvier Verlag, 1991) 599-611.

Introduction

Very little attention has been paid to Kant's treatment of happiness. This study aims to give a systematic account in Kant's terms of the role of happiness in ethics. Happiness must be considered in order to have a view of Kant's ethics which is complete and not overly simplistic. Kant's treatment of happiness does not consist of a random collection of statements; there is a method to Kant's treatment of happiness, although Kant himself does not explicitly lay it out. Happiness, I show, may have several distinct tasks in ethics and so Kant's treatment of happiness will be discussed in terms of these tasks.

Some readers of Kant have no doubt paid little attention to happiness in ethics because Kant says that "the concept of happiness is so indeterminate a concept" (Gr.85/4,418). It is true that we may not be able to say specifically what happiness is. Is it pleasure, health, good fortune, and so on? How much of each does it take to produce happiness? But we can say generally what happiness is and that goes a long way in helping us to understand Kant's ethics. We can say generally that happiness is the satisfaction of our inclinations (granted, we do not all have the same inclinations) and that happiness is not the same as moral contentment or bliss.

Similarly, it is not adequate to conclude that because Kant makes some negative claims about the value of happiness to ethics that happiness has no place in his ethics. Kant's ethic is an ethic of duty, of acting for the sake of the moral law, but that does not necessarily make it an ethic in which happiness has no place. Compare these claims:

1. a. The differentiation between these two [the doctrine of happiness and the doctrine of morality] is the

first and most important task charged to the Analytic of Pure Practical Reason (CPR,95/5,92).

b. Maxims of virtue and those of one's own happiness are wholly heterogeneous (CPR,117/5,112).

2. a. The system of morality is therefore inseparably—though only in the idea of pure reason—bound up with that of happiness (A809/B837).

b. Happiness is not a ground, not a principle of morality, but a necessary corollary of it (LE,78/M,97).

The first claims state that the doctrine of happiness and the doctrine of morality must be differentiated and that principles of happiness are completely unlike principles of morality. The second claims assert that the system of morality is tied to that of happiness and that happiness is a necessary corollary to principles of morality. The first claims seem to exclude happiness from morality (that is, to view happiness negatively) while the second claims tie happiness to morality (that is, treat happiness positively).

Obviously, Kant's account of happiness must be a complex one if it is consistent and if it has a context for the above claims. The argument to be made in this work is that Kant's treatment of happiness is basically consistent and is organized around four tasks happiness may perform in ethics. Happiness may be: a principle of ethics, a natural end of moral agents, a means to a moral end, or itself part of a moral end. By looking at these four possible tasks of happiness, I show that Kant considers the first task to be negative while the other three to a greater or lesser extent are positive. Hence, there is a system at work in Kant's claims about the role of happiness in ethics though he never elucidates it. That will be part of the job of this study.

There are also two significant conclusions which follow from the claim that Kant's account of happiness has a system and can be laid out in an organized way. These conclusions are never stated unequivocally by Kant. But since he does not make explicit the organizational scheme by which he considers happiness, we cannot expect him to have drawn any conclusions that follow from this scheme. Certainly, the conclusions stated here are unsupported and may seem shocking or non-Kantian. But both will be argued for in the body of the work.

The first conclusion is that for Kant ends always act as determining grounds of the will. Since every action has an end, every action takes its determining ground *at least in part* from its end. This means that moral actions are not distinguished from prudent actions in that the former have formal determining grounds (i.e., the law) and the latter have material determining grounds (i.e., an end). Rather moral actions have formal determining grounds and, in addition, material determining grounds. Moral actions also have specific kinds of material determining grounds. Ends act as determining grounds of the will but for moral acts, ends are not the sole determining ground. Instead, some types of ends can work in conjunction with, as corollaries to, formal determining grounds. This work considers the role of ends in Kant's ethics.

The second conclusion is that happiness is of value and plays a positive role in Kant's ethics. Happiness is not only not rejected by Kant's nonconsequentialist ethic, it is granted moral value. Thus, while happiness ought not serve as the ground of ethics or as a principle of ethics, it is of value in ethics as a natural end, as a means to a moral end, and as part of the highest moral end. Furthermore, human beings have, in both indirect and direct ways, a duty to pursue happiness. This work focuses on the positive treatment of happiness manifest in Kant's ethics.

Kant critics have taken basically two approaches to the issue of happiness in Kant's ethics. First, there is the view that happiness plays no role in Kant's ethics of duty. According to this view, "happiness is nothing." This means that Kant's ethic excludes, rejects, has nothing to do with the claims of happiness. This view is often expressed by saying that Kant's ethic is a pure ethic of duty, unconcerned with the objects or ends of the will. Second, there is the view that happiness is more important than anything else in Kant's ethics. According to this view, "happiness is everything." It is said that Kant's ethic is above all else concerned with happiness. Or again, it is claimed that Kant's ethic is teleological, concerned primarily with the objects or ends of the will.

The "happiness is nothing" interpretation of Kant's ethics is the most persistent of the two approaches, though many have spoken against it. Some of the earliest of Kant's commentators are credited with advancing this view, although the view is still prevalent today as evidenced especially by the authors of introductory textbooks. John R. Silber claims that Kant's contemporary, Garve, and Schopenhauer advanced the view that Kant accords no place for happiness in a moral life.[1] Silber notes that Kant responds to Garve in *Theory and Practice* by denying that the virtuous person must always take no regard for happiness (TP,48/8,281). Schopenhauer, says Silber, treated the *Groundwork* as Kant's complete work on ethics and so ignored other works concerned with the material of ethics. Schopenhauer then criticized Kant for failing to recognize the place of happiness in the moral life.[2]

Another critic who is credited with the view that happiness is unimportant to Kant is Schiller. Both Lewis White Beck and H. J. Paton state that, according to Schiller, Kant's emphasis on the rational in ethics serves to exclude happiness from ethics. Beck claims that Schiller is responsible for views about the "hardness" of Kant's idea of duty and about Kant's consequent ignoring of feelings and the sensuous in ethics.[3] Similarly, Paton says that it was Schiller who maintained that in Kantian ethics an act has no moral worth if inclination is present or if pleasure or satisfaction results from an act performed out of duty.[4] Beck and Paton, and also Silber, consider these early interpretations of Kant's ethics by

Garve, Schopenhauer, and Schiller to be misinterpretations.

Yet this view or misinterpretation has continued to be a part of discussions of Kant's ethics. There is still a need to call attention to this misinterpretation because it continues to seduce even those who have read Kant with more than superficial interest. It is certainly neat or simple to conclude that since Kant's ethic is an ethic of duty, it does not recognize a place for happiness, inclination, or the sensuous in ethics. However, this conclusion is not true.

H. H. Schroeder points out these misinterpretations of Kant in an article published in 1940 called, "Some Common Misinterpretations of the Kantian Ethics."[5] He asserts that it is incorrect to say that Kant condemns the inclinations or to say that morality has no connection with happiness.[6] Yet there are those who offer these views of Kant. Theodore M. Greene says, in his Introduction to Kant's *Religion*, that the moral law if it is pure must have nothing to do with happiness.[7] Edward Caird and A. C. Ewing are two others who are accused by Viggo Rossvaer of asserting that Kant's formalism entails a disregard of ends.[8] They claim that Kant's formal ethic ignores the place of ends in ethics.

There are also those textbook writers who foster this view that Kant's ethic excludes considerations of happiness and of ends. It has been claimed, for instance, that in Kant's ethics "the good will is the only thing that counts"[9] and therefore "we must avoid such ends and aims as happiness."[10] Another author has said that Kant "renders at least amoral the deepest yearnings of the human heart for its happiness and introduces a morality of such disinterestedness as to deny the reasonableness of any love of self."[11] Finally, it has been claimed that for Kant "morality is entirely separate from the pursuit of happiness."[12]

On the opposite side are those who argue that happiness is everything to Kant or that Kant's primary focus is on ends. This view is less popular than the view that happiness or ends mean nothing to Kant though it is no less extreme. Two proponents of this view are Thomas Auxter and Keith Ward. Both are concerned more with the issue of teleology than with happiness. Yet both conclude that Kant's ethics is focused primarily on the ends or objects of the will and since happiness is an object of the will, their claims about ends seem to have implications for happiness.

Auxter defines moral teleology as "the study of the objects of the moral will"[13] and he argues that moral teleology is central to Kant's practical philosophy.[14] Interestingly, in his talk of the objects and ends of the moral will, Auxter does not say much about the moral agent's own happiness. He even asserts that the highest good (happiness in accordance with virtue) ought not be the end of a moral will.[15] Thus, while Auxter believes that Kant's ethics is teleological and that ends are of primary importance, he does not reach any specific conclusions about the place of happiness. However, Keith Ward in emphasizing the teleological nature of Kant's ethic does reach such a conclusion. He says that Kant's ethic is a teleological ethic and that it is concerned "above all" with the ends of action and with happiness.[16] He concludes that Kant's "main ethical concern" was with human fulfillment and happiness and with the means for attaining it.[17]

Two others who focus on the content of Kant's ethics are Marcus Singer and Bruce Aune. Singer argues that Kant is not a formalist because the maxim of an action always possesses a content.[18] Hence, there is a necessary teleology in Kant's ethics, that is, a concern with the content, object, or end of the will. On this, Singer, Auxter, and Ward agree. Singer also argues that Kant appeals to consequences to help determine whether an act is right or wrong.[19] This is a claim about consequentialism. If true, it does refute Kant's formalism, but consequentialism does not follow necessarily from teleology. This investigation of Kant's ethics will show it to be teleological (concerned with ends) but will not consider the issue of consequentialism or what makes actions right. Finally, Bruce Aune also observes the teleological nature of Kant's ethics. However, he views this emphasis on teleology as a mistake on Kant's part. He claims that the central weakness of Kant's moral theory is its appeal to a teleological system of nature.[20]

Now what is extreme about these teleological interpretations of Kant's ethics, especially Auxter's and Ward's, is that they treat Kant's ethics as concerned centrally, above all else, and mainly with ends. While it is certainly true that Kant's ethics is concerned with ends, it is less obvious that his ethics is concerned *above all else* with ends. This study shows that Kant's ethics is concerned (though not above all else) with one end at least, the end of happiness.

A major weakness in the claims of both these opposing groups is that no one in either group has systematically laid out and evaluated Kant's claims about happiness. All have reached conclusions about the place of happiness (or, in some cases, of ends) without considering thoroughly Kant's assertions about happiness. Viggo Rossvaer says this about the *Groundwork*, though it applies as well to all of Kant's works on ethics: "The concept of happiness appears in many places and in many connections throughout *Grundlegung*, although it is not itself thoroughly analysed."[21] The point is that before either approach—"happiness is nothing"/"happiness is everything"—can be said to be "right," it is crucial to look carefully at what Kant says about happiness.

In spite of this deficiency, one of these two approaches is more true to Kant (i.e., correct) than the other. It is more true of Kant's ethics to say "happiness is everything" than it is to say "happiness is nothing." Neither statement is perfectly true of Kant's ethics since both need to be qualified. "Happiness is (almost) everything" if we consider happiness in its role as means to morality or in its role as part of a moral end. "Happiness is nothing" if we consider happiness in its role as principle for action. Thus, I look at what happiness does in

Kant's ethics before judging how important it is to his ethics. By isolating the four tasks Kant assigns to happiness, it will be clear in what respect happiness plays no role in ethics and in what respects happiness plays a vital role in ethics. This study shows that there are several significant respects in which happiness is crucial to ethics and hence, that if we must pick sides, it is more correct to say "happiness is everything" (almost everything) than it is to say "happiness is nothing."

As an indication of the importance of happiness in Kant's ethics, consider the following passage. Happiness cannot be "nothing" in Kant's ethics because when Kant speaks of morality he seems to feel a certain necessity to speak also of happiness.

> The moral law contains within it a natural promise of happiness: it tells me that if I conduct myself so as to be worthy of happiness I may hope for it; here are the springs of morality and morality thus has a necessary relation to happiness (LE,77-78/M,97).

The relationship between morality and happiness is too complex to be resolved by a simple denial of any such connection.

Two Kant commentators come close to recognizing the importance of happiness in Kant's ethics. John Silber and John Atwell both avoid the extreme interpretations in which Kant's ethic is said to ignore happiness and ends or to be concerned primarily with happiness and ends. Silber speaks against the view that Kant ignores happiness and refers instead to Kant's insistence on "the goodness of happiness."[22] He speaks too of the importance of the highest good to Kant's practical philosophy.[23] Yet, when Silber discusses the ways in which happiness is good, he focuses on happiness as a natural end, as a nonmoral value. When he speaks of happiness as part of the highest good, he sometimes speaks of it as only the happiness of others.[24] This study looks at how happiness is good as a natural end but in addition it considers how happiness, the moral agent's own happiness, becomes the object of a moral duty, and, in fact, a part of a moral end.

Atwell believes that the teleological dimension of Kant's thought is often overlooked.[25] But in his desire to bring to light Kant's teleology, Atwell does not deny Kant's formalism.[26] Atwell sees Kant's emphasis on teleology, on ends, on happiness, as one part of Kant's ethics but as an emphasis that does not exclude a concern for the formality and the purity of moral principles. Hence, for Atwell, ends and happiness are important to Kant but not important above all else. While Atwell treats the more general issue of the role of ends in Kant's ethic, this study focuses on the role of happiness in Kant's ethic.

I proceed in this way. Chapter 1 considers Kant's definition of happiness, that is, what happiness is. Chapters 2-6 discuss what happiness does in Kant's ethics, that is, the possible roles to be played by happiness in ethics. Chapter 2 considers happiness as a principle of ethics. Chapter 3 considers happiness as a natural end of moral agents. Chapter 4 treats happiness as a means to a moral end. Chapters 5 and 6 treat happiness as itself part of a moral end (the highest good). Kant speaks, albeit not directly, of these four possible tasks for happiness in ethics and concludes that happiness is something negative, something to be excluded from morality, only in its first task as principle of ethics. In its other three roles, as natural end, as means to a moral end, as itself part of a moral end, happiness is something positive, something of value, and even in some cases, something we ought to pursue on moral grounds. In this way then, the work considers the place of happiness in Kant's ethics and in particular emphasizes the positive roles of happiness in Kant's ethics.

Chapter One

The Definition of Happiness

I begin by looking at Kant's descriptions of happiness [*Glückseligkeit*]. While Kant uses many different terms in his discussions of happiness (for example, well-being, contentment, inclination, pleasure, bliss), there are two fundamentally different ways he considers happiness.[1] On the one hand, Kant treats happiness as a sensible state, that is, as a state that involves the satisfaction of inclinations, brings pleasure, and is characterized as well-being.[2] On the other hand, Kant describes happiness as an intelligible state, that is, as a state that involves moral contentment.[3] He sometimes calls the first "physical happiness" and the second "moral happiness." I explore the way in which happiness is sensible or physical in section I. Of particular importance to this description of happiness are the terms "inclination" and "pleasure." In section II, I consider happiness as intelligible or moral. Here the terms "moral happiness," "self-contentment" and "bliss" are important. Finally, in section III, I reach a conclusion concerning which of these two accounts of happiness best reflects Kant's understanding of happiness (granted that he speaks of happiness in both ways). I also suggest how these descriptions of happiness are tied to a problem in Kant's account of the highest good.

I. Happiness As Sensible

While there are unclarities in Kant's notion of happiness, there is no doubt that he thought of happiness as a physical state. In several places, Kant uses the terms "well-being" and "welfare" to describe happiness. In the *Groundwork*, Kant says that complete well-being [*Wohlbefinden*] and contentment [*Zufriedenheit*] with one's state is called happiness [*Glückseligkeit*] (Gr.61/4,393). Further he observes that a person's preservation [*Erhaltung*] or welfare [*Wohlergehen*] is "in a word his happiness [*Glückseligkeit*]" (Gr.63/4,395). In the second *Critique*, happiness [*Glückseligkeit*] is said to be a person's "consciousness of the agreeableness of life [*das Bewusstsein . . . von der Annehmlichkeit des Lebens*] which without interruption accompanies his whole existence" (CPR,20/5,22). "Happiness [*Glückseligkeit*] is the condition of a rational being in the world, in whose whole existence everything goes according to wish and will" (CPR,129/5,124). Happiness [*Glückseligkeit*], in the *Metaphysics of Morals*, is said to be "satisfaction [*Zufriedenheit*] with one's condition . . . with what nature bestows" (MM,45/6,387). Elsewhere, Kant states that happiness [*Glückseligkeit*] contains whatever nature can obtain for us (TP,50n/8,283). Happiness [*Glückseligkeit*] refers to "constant well-being [*Wohlergehen*], a pleasant life, complete satisfaction [*Zufriedenheit*] with one's condition" (MM,149/6,480). The *Lectures on Ethics* also describes happiness [*Glückseligkeit*] as well-being [*Wohlbefinden*] and identifies this well-being with "the physical good [*das physische Gut*]" (LE,8/M,10). Thus, *Glückseligkeit* is happiness and it has to do with the state of a person's life in the natural world. A person's happiness has to do with his or her preservation, welfare, and well-being; in short, with the condition of his or her sensible life.

Because happiness means a pleasant life, satisfaction with a person's own physical state, it is called a physical good. Kant names one element of the highest good "well-being" (what he elsewhere calls happiness) and labels it the physical good. He states that the highest physical good is happiness [*Glückseligkeit*] (CJ,301/5,450). Kant explains that human beings desire happiness because their nature is such that they are dependent on circumstances of sensibility (Rel.41-42n/6,46). He adds that human beings cannot be expected to wholly renounce what is physical in happiness (Rel.125/6,135). Clearly, happiness operates in these passages as a physical good, as an object desired because human beings are sensible beings.

Kant even at times refers to this physical good as "physical happiness." He describes physical happiness [*physische Glückseligkeit*] as the possession of contentment with one's physical state [*Zufriedenheit mit seinem physischen Zustande*] (Rel.61/6,67) and as satisfaction with what nature bestows [*Zufriedenheit mit . . . was die Natur beschert*] (MM,45/6,387).[4] In these passages, Kant attaches the term "physical" to happiness as a qualifier. He intends thereby to distinguish one sort of happiness, physical happiness, from another sort of happiness which he calls "moral happiness" (see section II). Thus, in this first sense of happiness, happiness has to do with the state of a human being's life in the sensible world.

There are certainly differences among the passages above that purport to offer an account of happiness as a sensible state. Some of the passages claim directly that happiness is well-being or a pleasant life. Other passages say that happiness is a person's satisfaction with his or her physical state.[5] It seems that happiness is said to be both the physical state itself and the person's satisfaction with that physical state. Surely, these are different. To say happiness is a pleasant life is different than saying happiness is a person's consciousness of the agreeableness of life. Perhaps the point here is that a person cannot be happy without being conscious of being happy. Perhaps it is not enough to have a pleasant life unless a human being knows he or she is having a pleasant life. In this sense, happiness goes beyond the mere presence of a certain sensible state to an awareness and a satisfaction with that state. Happiness possibly requires both well-being and satisfaction with that state of well-being. But, based on the evidence there is,

Kant does not explicitly make this point. He speaks more loosely of happiness both as well-being (a state of affairs in nature) and as satisfaction with that well-being (an attitude towards a state of affairs in nature).[6]

It is possible too that there may be a disparity between a state of nature and a person's contentment with that state of nature. One person may be content with a certain level of well-being with which another person is not content. Are both happy? That depends on whether happiness is the state itself or our satisfaction with the state. Both may have the same pleasant life though one fails to be satisfied with that life. If happiness is the having of a pleasant life, then both have realized happiness. But, if happiness requires satisfaction with the conditions of a person's life, then only the first person has realized happiness. A person may not be satisfied with his or her sensible condition even though it is an extremely pleasant life, according to others. Or, a person may be satisfied with his or her sensible condition even though it is not a very pleasant life, according to others. Hence, it is not obvious that there is any clear relationship between a level of well-being and a person's satisfaction with that level of well-being.

However, one point remains. Both of these descriptions of happiness—as a pleasant life and as satisfaction with that life—have to do with our physical state. Though Kant describes happiness as both well-being and as contentment [*Zufriedenheit*] with one's condition, both of these accounts look to our condition in nature, to the fact of our existence in the sensible world.[7] Neither description postpones happiness to another world or considers happiness to be in principle unreachable in the sensible world. Neither account treats happiness as if it were independent of or had nothing to do with our sensible nature. Therefore, on the central point, there is no difficulty. Kant uses the term "happiness" to describe a sensible state and/or our satisfaction with a sensible state. Happiness concerns a physical state of affairs. Because happiness is a physical state or an attitude towards a physical state, happiness is a goal to be achieved in the sensible world.

Next, happiness is defined in terms of inclination as evidenced by Kant's repeated linking of the two terms. He claims that reason does not approve of happiness (though inclination [*Neigung*] may desire it) except when it is combined with worthiness to be happy (A813/B841). He insists that an action done from duty must ignore the influence of inclination [*den Einfluss der Neigung*] (Gr.68/4,400). Yet he acknowledges that a person's needs and inclinations [*seinen Bedürfnissen und Neigungen*] (whose satisfaction is happiness) run counter to the commands of duty (Gr.73/4,405). Thus, inclination is a kind of motivating force like reason. It aims to determine the will in ways opposite to reason (based on subjective rather than objective conditions). Inclination refers to the dependency of the will on sensations and subjective conditions. Inclination indicates a need (Gr.81n/4,414) and influences the will to aim at satisfying that sensible need. Inclination directs reason to formulate principles for its service, principles aimed thus at the satisfying of needs. Happiness is the satisfaction of these needs and inclinations. Presumably, a person has numerous inclinations (for instance, needs for health, wealth, fame, and so on). When these inclinations are satisfied, when the person has a pleasant life, the person is happy.

Even though, according to Kant, happiness is the satisfaction of inclinations, there is still uncertainty concerning what this means. Commentators have argued quite rightly that Kant speaks of two ways in which the satisfaction of inclinations, that is, happiness, may be accomplished.[8] Kant's statements about happiness seem to refer both to the satisfaction of *all* inclinations and to the satisfaction of a complex *system* of inclinations (a hierarchy of inclinations). Kant does not explicitly make this distinction or argue for one interpretation over the other, although his texts reveal both of these views.

On the one hand, there are passages in which Kant speaks of happiness as the satisfaction of all inclinations. Kant states that "happiness consists in the satisfaction of *all* our inclinations [*aller Neigungen*]" (LE,38/M,47); "Happiness is the satisfaction of *all* our desires [*aller unserer Neigungen*]" (A806/B834); and "in this Idea of happiness *all* inclinations [*alle Neigungen*] are combined into a sum total" (Gr.67/4,399).[9] In other texts, he reiterates: "the sum of *all* inclinations [*aller Neigungen*], i.e. happiness" (CJ,284n/5,434n);[10] and "there is required for the Idea of happiness an absolute whole, a maximum of well-being" (Gr.85/4,418).[11] All of these passages focus on the number of inclinations to be satisfied—all, sum total, maximum. According to this definition of happiness, there is a collection of inclinations, the sum total of which must be realized, in order for happiness to be achieved.

On the other hand, there are passages in which Kant speaks of happiness as the satisfaction of a system of inclinations. Kant refers to: "All inclinations taken together (which can be brought into a fairly tolerable system [*System*], whereupon their satisfaction is called happiness" (CPR,75-76/5,73). He states that: "Natural inclinations . . . can be brought into harmony in a wholeness [*Zusammenstimmung in einem Ganzen*] which is called happiness" (Rel.51/6,58). These passages focus on the harmonizing and systematizing of inclinations. They suggest that happiness refers not to the satisfying of all inclinations but to the satisfying of an organized system of inclinations.

Now several questions may be raised: Are these views of happiness incompatible or can they be reconciled? Is there any indication that Kant preferred one view to another?

There is at least in theory a difference between satisfying all inclinations and satisfying a system of inclinations. "All inclinations" refers to the number of inclinations to be realized while "a system of inclinations" refers to the way in which the inclinations are to be realized. For example, to realize all of a person's inclinations is to satisfy those inclinations in no particular order and according to no particular scheme. If happiness is the satisfaction of all inclinations, then there is no discrimination among inclinations (none is apparently better or worse than any other) and it is not necessary to forego satisfying one inclination in order to satisfy another (all are to be satisfied). The satisfaction of all inclinations excludes the notion of a system of inclinations. All seems to mean that no inclination takes priority; none must come before another. However, the satisfaction of a system of inclinations does not preclude realizing all inclinations. It may be that all inclinations are still realized only now in a particular order and according to a particular scheme. Or the notion of a system could mean that the satisfaction of all inclinations is not possible. A person may have to forego satisfying one inclination in order to satisfy another inclination or the system of inclinations. In a system, it is possible to discriminate among inclinations; some inclinations may be more valuable than others.

Thus, in theory, there is a difference between these two views of happiness. Happiness as the satisfaction of all inclinations excludes the notion of happiness as the satisfaction of a system of inclinations. But happiness as the satisfaction of a system of inclinations need not exclude the notion of happiness as the satisfaction of all inclinations. These views of happiness need not be incompatible (a system of inclinations can include all inclinations) but they may be incompatible (a system of inclinations may not include all inclinations and all inclinations excludes a system of inclinations). Hence, there is no contradiction between Kant's definitions of happiness if it can be assumed that he intends happiness to be the satisfaction of a system of inclinations which includes all inclinations.

Yet, Kant considers two difficulties that concern any definition of happiness which includes the satisfaction of all inclinations. The first difficulty has to do with the possibility of realizing all inclinations. Kant says that all inclinations means "an infinite number of inclinations" and that it is unlikely that this infinite number of inclinations could ever be satisfied. Kant states that it is vain to expect that imperatives aimed at happiness could attain "the totality of a series of consequences which is in fact infinite" (Gr.86/4,419). A definition of happiness that includes the satisfying of all inclinations has to include all present and future inclinations (Gr.85/4,418). So, Kant concludes that there is a problem both in determining what is included in all inclinations and in aiming to realize all inclinations.

The second difficulty concerns whether or not happiness can in fact be said to be the satisfaction of all inclinations. Here Kant seems to argue against the view that happiness is the satisfaction of all inclinations. He claims that the "prescription for happiness is, however, often so constituted as greatly to interfere with some inclinations" (Gr.67/4,399). Kant gives the example of a person suffering from gout. He says that such a person may choose to satisfy a single inclination rather than the "wavering Idea" of happiness, since the former is determinate regarding what it promises and the time of its satisfaction.[12] A person may decide to forego the pursuit of happiness as a whole in order to satisfy a relatively certain particular inclination, since otherwise this particular inclination may be frustrated in the pursuit of the whole. The gout-sufferer desires a certain food but desires health. If, as Kant says here, the pursuit of happiness interferes with the satisfying of some inclinations, then obviously, happiness cannot be the satisfying of all inclinations. Happiness understood as the satisfaction of all inclinations cannot account for the gout-sufferer or for the possibility of incompatible inclinations.

These two difficulties suggest that happiness is best understood as the realization of a system of inclinations. Both of the problems Kant raises concerning the definition of happiness have to do with happiness as the satisfaction of all inclinations. Because Kant offers no objections to the second definition of happiness as the satisfaction of a system of inclinations, it seems to be the more acceptable view.[13]

However, the difficulties Kant has considered imply that the earlier attempt to bring together the two definitions of happiness does not work. The argument there was that the two definitions of happiness need not be incompatible in that a system of inclinations may include all inclinations. It now seems that Kant does not mean for a system of inclinations to include all inclinations. He recognizes that the system which is happiness excludes the satisfying of certain inclinations. Thus, the system which is happiness does not include all inclinations and so the two definitions of happiness are incompatible and cannot be brought together. Hence, there is some evidence that Kant found more acceptable the notion that happiness is the satisfaction of a system of inclinations though this conclusion is challenged by his frequent defining of happiness as the satisfaction of all inclinations.

Finally, happiness is defined in terms of pleasure [*Lust*].[14] Kant offers a series of examples in the second *Critique* which are similar to the gout-sufferer example in the *Groundwork*. In both places, Kant considers a person who desires two objects and makes a choice between them. If a person's desire for some object (his/her inclination) is to be the determining ground of the will, then the choice of this or that object will depend on feelings of agreeableness (how certain is the pleasure to be received from this object, how immediate, etc.). In these examples, the notions of happiness and inclination are tied to notions of agreeableness and pleasure. Kant says:

> A man can return unread an instructive book which he cannot again obtain, in order not to miss the hunt; he can go away in the middle of a fine speech, in order not to be late for a meal; he can leave an intellectual conversation, which he otherwise enjoys, in order to take his place at the gambling table; he can even repulse a poor man

> whom it is usually a joy to aid, because he has only enough money in his pocket for a ticket to the theater (CPR,22/5,23).

In one sense, these examples are like the example of the gout-sufferer. When a person is "pathologically determined," when a person acts in order to achieve some end, the principle on which the person acts cannot be a practical law because it is not universal. We cannot determine which of two desired objects a person ought to have acted to realize. Even less can we determine which objects all people ought to act to realize. Kant's point is that there is no difference in kind between the objects at issue in these examples. Whether the gout-sufferer eats this food or aims to achieve happiness, whether a person reads an instructive book or attends the hunt; in all cases these choices are choices between two desired objects, either of which might serve as determining ground of the will. Neither choice is moral, neither is based on a practical law, because in both cases, the action is based on desire for some object and it matters not the nature of the object. So these examples all show that insofar as an object of desire is the determining ground of the will, the moral value of the action is the same. We cannot discriminate between "higher" and "lower" objects of desire. Happiness is not necessarily to be preferred to a certain food and an instructive book is not necessarily to be preferred to the hunt. Which object acts to determine a person's will depends on the inclinations and the pleasures of the person and it is thus futile to try to prescribe which objects ought to be desired.

In another sense, these examples differ from the example of the gout-sufferer. In these examples, a person is choosing between two particular objects; for example, a book and a hunt. In the example of the gout-sufferer, a person is choosing between a particular food and happiness as a whole. The former examples reveal a conflict between individual objects of inclination while the latter example shows that an individual object of inclination may conflict with the system of inclinations. Both examples show that our desires to achieve certain sensible ends may be incompatible although only the latter shows that our desire to achieve a certain sensible end may be incompatible with our desire to achieve a system of sensible ends.

These examples also serve to link happiness and inclination to pleasure. Happiness is a rational being's consciousness of the agreeableness of life [*Annehmlichkeit des Lebens*] (CPR,20/5,22). The principle of happiness includes all principles which place the determining ground of the will in the pleasure [*Lust*] or displeasure received from an object (CPR,20-21/5,22). Kant insists that a man who is concerned only with the agreeableness of life (i.e., happiness) asks only how much and how great is the pleasure [*Vergnügen*] which this or that object might bring him (CPR,22/5,23). He says: "Where one places his happiness is a question of the particular feeling of pleasure [*Lust*] or displeasure in each man" (CPR,24/5,25). Finally, he claims that happiness is "always pleasant [*angenehm*] to him who possesses it" (CPR,115/5,111). Happiness then has to do with the agreeableness of life and happiness is to be found in realizing those objects which bring pleasure. Principles of happiness aim at the maximizing of pleasure.

There are several other passages in which Kant links happiness to agreeableness and pleasure. He describes happiness as the "greatest sum of the pleasantness of life [*Annehmlichkeiten des Lebens*]" (CJ,42/5,208) and refers to happiness "with the whole abundance of its pleasures [*Annehmlichkeit*]" (CJ,43/5,209). He tells us: "Pleasantness [*Annehmlichkeit*] is enjoyment [*Genuss*]" (CJ,42/5,208) and "That which pleases the senses in sensation is 'pleasant' [*Angenehm*]" (CJ,39/5,205). Kant distinguishes the pleasant from the beautiful and the good and relates it to inclination. Thus, he speaks of "the interest of inclination [*Neigung*] in the case of the pleasant [*Angenehmen*]" (CJ,44/5,210).

In the *Groundwork* too, Kant distinguishes between the pleasant and the good. The pleasant, he says, influences the will solely through sensation (Gr.81/4,413). The dependence of a will on sensations is called an inclination and in this case a person is oriented towards the *object* of the action (so far as the object is pleasant to the person) (Gr.81n/4,413-14n). Kant claims in another place that if the doctrine of morals were nothing but a doctrine of happiness then there would be no need of a priori principles. Reason cannot determine "by what means one could attain a lasting enjoyment [*Genuss*] of the true pleasures of life [*Freuden des Lebens*]" (MM,14/6,215). Only experience is truly helpful in making a person's "choice of a way of life suitable to his particular inclination [*Neigung*] and susceptibility for pleasure [*Vergnügen*]" (MM,14-15/6,216).

It is clear that Kant often links pleasure and pleasantness to happiness. Happiness has to do with the agreeableness of life which in turn is defined by how much pleasure is provided. Similarly, principles of happiness aim to satisfy particular inclinations. They are directed towards "the pleasant." Kant uses several words for pleasure or pleasantness (among them; *Annehmlichkeit, Lust, Vergnügen, Angenehm, Freuden*). But he does not seem to be concerned to distinguish among them. Neither is he concerned to establish precisely the connection between happiness and pleasure. Happiness involves the satisfaction of inclinations and inclinations are directed towards achieving what is pleasant. Kant is talking both about what happiness is and how principles of happiness operate. Perhaps that is one reason why the relationship between happiness and pleasure is not spelled out in detail. Principles of happiness are based on inclination and desire for some object and thus are directed toward what is pleasant, what brings pleasure. But it is another thing to say that happiness is the satisfaction of inclinations and thus is pleasant, or is pleasure. For instance, what would we make of Kant's example of the gout-sufferer who chooses the pleasure of a certain food over the pleasure of happiness, if happiness is equated with pleasure or with what is pleasant.

This section has not resolved all of the difficulties in Kant's definition of happiness as inclination and pleasure. Probably, it is not possible to do so. What this section has shown is that Kant considers happiness to involve a physical state in the natural world. There is a connection between happiness and pleasure, inclination, and sensation. When the will is determined to act for the end of happiness, the will is dependent on sensation, and it acts to satisfy inclinations and achieve pleasure. This notion of what happiness is and what happiness involves treats happiness as a sensible state.

II. Happiness As Intelligible

There are three other descriptions Kant gives of happiness. These descriptions stand apart from the previous account of happiness in that they seem to consider happiness to be a mental state or a person's consciousness of himself or herself as a moral agent or a state to be realized in a future world. These three descriptions are alike in that each denies that happiness is a sensible state that occurs when inclinations are satisfied and pleasures are realized. To be considered are Kant's discussions of: moral happiness [*moralische Glückseligkeit*], moral contentment or self-contentment [*Zufriedenheit*], and bliss [*Seligkeit*].

Kant seems to suggest that happiness can be a mental state when he distinguishes moral happiness [*moralische Glückseligkeit*] from physical happiness [*physische Glückseligkeit*] in *Religion* and in the *Metaphysics of Morals*. If happiness can be "moral," then it need not be a sensible state having to do with inclination and pleasure. In *Religion*, he claims that by moral happiness he means "the reality and *constancy* of a disposition which ever progresses in goodness (and never falls away from it)" (Rel.61/6,67). This happiness is not "that assurance of the everlasting possession of contentment with one's *physical state* (freedom from evils and enjoyment of ever-increasing pleasures) which is *physical happiness*" (Rel.61/6,67). Rather, moral happiness "consists of a consciousness of progress in goodness" (Rel.69n/6,75n).

In the *Metaphysics of Morals*, Kant mentions the possibility of thinking "a certain moral happiness [*moralische Glückseligkeit*] not resting on empirical causes" (MM,33/6,377). He continues:

> When the thinking man has triumphed over temptations to vice and is conscious of having done his often difficult duty, he finds himself in a state of satisfaction [*Zufriedenheit*] and peace of mind which can well be called happiness [*den man gar wohl Glückseligkeit nennen kann*] (MM,33/6,377).

> Some people still make a distinction between moral and physical happiness [*moralischen und physischen Glückseligkeit*] (the former consisting in satisfaction [*Zufriedenheit*] with one's own person and moral conduct, and thus with what one does; the other in satisfaction with what nature bestows, and hence with what one enjoys as an external gift) (MM,45/6,387).

In these passages, Kant seems to be admitting that there is a kind of happiness called moral happiness which is the contentment that follows from doing one's duty or progressing in goodness. Moral happiness proposes a kind of happiness that is not sensible and does not have to do with inclination or pleasure. But there are several reasons for insisting that Kant's aim is not to posit such a moral happiness. This can be shown by reconsidering the above passages, emphasizing certain terms and looking at phrases previously omitted.

In terms of what the passages say, there are two important qualifications. Kant speaks of the possibility of *thinking* a *certain* moral happiness which *can well be called* happiness. This is far from stating that there *is* a kind of happiness which is moral happiness. Also he says that *some people* still make a distinction between moral and physical happiness. Kant seems to be simply reporting facts about what can possibly be thought and what some people think. He is not offering a defense of this distinction. These qualifications suggest that Kant is not committed to the claim that moral happiness is a kind of happiness. If there were any further doubt, the following makes it clear that Kant is not proposing there is such a thing as moral happiness.

In both of the above passages, Kant goes on to make a judgment about the concept of moral happiness. He calls the concept of moral happiness "a self-contradictory nonentity [*ein sich selbst widersprechendes Unding*]" (MM,33/6,377) and claims that the term "contains a contradiction [*einen Widerspruch in sich enthält*]" (MM,45/6,387). Though Kant is willing to note that the concept of moral happiness has a definition, he is unwilling to defend such a notion of happiness, and, in fact, thinks it is contradictory. Thus, the references in Kant's texts to moral happiness in no way support the idea that there is a kind of happiness which is intelligible or mental. Kant rejects the concept of moral happiness on grounds that a happiness which is not grounded on empirical causes contradicts the general definition of happiness which refers to a sensible state of affairs.

Next, there is an important ethical fragment in which Kant links happiness to moral contentment [*Zufriedenheit*].[15] This fragment seems to make happiness an intelligible or moral state or at the very least it makes happiness dependent on a prior intelligible or moral state. Kant apparently identifies happiness with an intelligible or moral state in these passages. "Happiness is not something sensed but something thought" (S,129/19,278). Persons have the ability "to create happiness even without the comforts of life" and this, he says, "is the intellectual (aspect of happiness)" (ibid.). Hence, "happiness is a product of one's own human reason" (S,130/19,282). These claims certainly make happiness an intelligible and not a sensible state.

In other passages, Kant establishes a more explicit connection between happiness and moral contentment. Here he maintains that happiness is derived from or conditioned by a person's contentment with his or her moral state. He says, "happiness must be derived from an a priori basis approved by reason" (S,128/19,277). So, there is "a certain stock of contentment [*Zufriedenheit*] necessary and indispensable, without which no happiness is possible" (ibid.,278). Kant also speaks several times about "the principle of self-contentment [*Selbstzufriedenheit*]" as "the condition" or "the formal condition" for all happiness (ibid.,280-81). According to these claims, happiness is conditioned by self-contentment and is a product of reason.

Clearly, in this fragment, Kant defines happiness at least partially in terms of morality. There is not here a strict separation between happiness and virtue. Self-contentment, the satisfaction people take in being moral agents and in having acted morally, is a condition for happiness and so links happiness and morality. Happiness, if it involves self-contentment, would have an intellectual, moral aspect, and could not be defined simply in terms of the sensible realm.

Yet, there are two reasons to be cautious about concluding that Kant identifies happiness with an intelligible state of self-contentment or even that he considers moral contentment to be a condition of happiness. First, in terms of what this fragment says, there is no identification of happiness and self-contentment. Kant says happiness is not possible without self-contentment and that there is an intellectual aspect of happiness. The passage does not say that self-contentment is happiness. Nevertheless, even if moral contentment is only a condition of happiness, it connects happiness to the intelligible realm. It ties happiness to morality in a way that goes beyond any definition of happiness as a sensible state or as satisfaction with a sensible state.

However, this fragment provides the only evidence there is that Kant thought of self-contentment as a condition for happiness. L. W. Beck does not consider the Reflexion to be representative of Kant's critical writings on ethics.[16] Certainly, given all the indications there are from Kant's critical and later works that happiness involves a sensible state, I believe we must dismiss this early attempt to link moral contentment and happiness.

Second, there is strong evidence in Kant's later works that he did not consider happiness to be equivalent to or even tied to moral contentment. In the *Groundwork*, Kant observes that "the more a cultivated reason concerns itself with the aim of enjoying life and happiness [*Glückseligkeit*], the farther does man get away from true contentment [*wahren Zufriedenheit*]" (Gr.63/4,395). Reason however in attaining its end, the establishment of a good will, is capable of its own kind of contentment [*Zufriedenheit*], that is, "contentment in fulfilling a purpose which in turn is determined by reason alone, even if this fulfilment should often involve interference with the purposes of inclination" (Gr.64/4,396). Thus, there is a kind of contentment which comes from having acted morally and this contentment is distinct from and often interferes with happiness.

In the second *Critique*, Kant makes a similar point. He asks whether we have a word to describe that negative satisfaction with existence which accompanies the consciousness of virtue. He answers: "We do, and this word is 'self-contentment' [*Selbstzufriedenheit*]" (CPR,122/5,117). He calls this self-contentment "an analogue of happiness" though he says it arises from the consciousness that we are free in obeying the moral law.[17] This self-contentment may be called intellectual [*intellectuell*] contentment and it is to be distinguished from a sensuous [*ästhetische*] contentment which arises from the satisfaction of inclinations (CPR,122/5,118). The latter, Kant says, "can never be adequate to that which is conceived under contentment" (ibid.). Thus, the contentment that results from the consciousness of a person's capacity to follow the moral law is different from the contentment or satisfaction that results when inclinations are satisfied. The former is self-contentment, the latter is happiness.

There are two ways of making explicit the distinction between self-contentment and the contentment which is happiness. The first is to note that self-contentment is always a product of freedom or morality unlike the contentment which is happiness. Kant claims that the source of self-contentment is "contentment with one's own person [*Zufriedenheit mit seiner Person*]" (CPR,123/5,118) and the consciousness "of freedom in obeying . . . moral maxims" (CPR,122/5,117). Happiness on the other hand rests on the satisfaction of inclinations and contentment with what nature bestows, with one's sensible condition (Gr.61/4,393; MM,45/6,387). Happiness is sometimes described as contentment, but it is clear that it is not equivalent to self-contentment given that the causes of these two contentments are different. Perhaps, as Kant suggests, self-contentment can be said to be "an analogue of happiness" but certainly the two are not identical.

Kant offers a second way of distinguishing between self-contentment and happiness when he labels the former "negative" satisfaction. Self-contentment refers to a negative satisfaction [*ein negatives Wohlgefallen*] with one's condition (CPR,123/5,118) in which one is conscious of needing nothing (CPR,122/5,117). Self-contentment rests on no particular feeling (ibid.). Inner satisfaction is merely negative with reference to everything which might make life pleasant (CPR,91/5,88). However, happiness indicates a gratification (CPR,122/5,117) and depends upon a positive participation of feeling (CPR,123/5,118). Hence, Kant concludes that the comfort that comes from acting morally "is not happiness, not even the smallest part of happiness" (CPR,91/5,88). Thus, self-contentment and happiness are not equivalent or necessarily linked because the former is a negative satisfaction (the state of recognizing no needs or ignoring needs) and the latter is a positive satisfaction (the state of gratifying needs).

Finally, there are indications in Kant's works that suggest he identifies happiness and bliss (*Seligkeit*). For instance, in the Preface to the *Metaphysics of Morals*, Kant shows the contradiction in the thinking of the eudaemonist and, in doing so, he seems to use happiness and bliss as synonyms. Kant says that for the eudaemonist, the motive for acting virtuously is the satisfaction that comes from doing one's duty, that is, "this bliss, this happiness" (MM,33/6,377). Hence, according to the eudaemonist, a person performs his or her duty only when the person foresees he or she will thereby be happy. But Kant points out it is only when a person observes duty that he or she can "hope to be happy [*glücklich*] (or inwardly blissful [*selig*])" (MM,34/6,377). Here happiness and bliss are taken to refer to the same state.

In another place, when Kant considers the ideal of holiness, he states that this ideal contains the strongest motive "that of happiness beyond this world" and he refers to this motive as "that of happiness [*Glückseligkeit*] or blessedness [*Seligkeit*]" (LE,10/M,13). In discussing the doctrine of Christianity, Kant claims that the well-being proportionate to holiness of morals which is bliss [*Seligkeit*] stands "under the name of happiness [*Glückseligkeit*]" and is thought of as attainable only in eternity (CPR,133/5,128-29).

These passages suggest that happiness can be described as bliss. In one sense, the strong sense, happiness and bliss seem to be synonyms. Bliss is offered as an explanation of the meaning of happiness. In another sense, the weak sense, bliss does not explain happiness, rather it is one kind of happiness and so it stands under the name of happiness. In this case, bliss refers to a happiness beyond this world.

Kant describes bliss in these ways. "Blessed" designates "a perfect well-being independent of all contingent causes in the world" (CPR,128n/5,123n). A bliss or an inborn possession would "presuppose a consciousness of our self-sufficiency" (CPR,24/5,25). Given this account of bliss as a state of independence from the sensible world and given Kant's earlier discussion of happiness as a sensible state involving inclination, it is impossible to argue that bliss and happiness are synonyms. Indeed, Kant says clearly that happiness or contentment with our existence "is not . . . an inborn possession or a bliss" (ibid.). At best, the weaker sense of connection, that makes bliss one type of happiness, is possible. Perhaps bliss is one kind of happiness; a happiness beyond this world, a happiness in eternity, a happiness in having done a person's duty. Exactly what Kant means by such a happiness beyond this world is not known nor is it clear by what right such a state can be called happiness. But it is clear that although Kant sometimes identifies happiness and bliss, they cannot be equated. If it is acceptable to allow for various types of happiness (and it is not at all clear that it is) then bliss may be named such a type, just as may moral happiness and self-contentment. To employ a term that Kant uses in regard to self-contentment, bliss may be an "analogue" of happiness. It is like happiness in that it is a state of well-being but it is unlike happiness in that the cause or source of it is different than that of happiness.

III. Conclusions and Implications

The previous section considered descriptions of three separate states which are similar to and sometimes identified with the state of happiness. Although Kant occasionally calls moral happiness, self-contentment, and bliss happiness, none of these states is in a strict sense happiness. This argument was made on the basis of Kant's claims themselves. Now, there is one more passage in which Kant differentiates among these states in a way that is helpful to understanding their relationship.

In a passage in the second *Critique*, Kant distinguishes self-contentment, happiness, and bliss. He says:

> we can understand how the consciousness of this capacity of a pure practical reason through a deed (virtue) can produce a consciousness of mastery over inclinations and thus of independence from them . . . bringing forth a negative satisfaction with one's condition, i.e., contentment [*Zufriedenheit*], whose source is contentment with one's own person . . . This cannot be called happiness [*Glückseligkeit*], since it does not depend upon a positive participation of feeling; nor can it be called bliss [*Seligkeit*], because it does not include complete independence from inclinations and desires. It does nevertheless resemble the latter . . . and thus, at least in its origin, it is analogous to the self-sufficiency which can be ascribed only to the Supreme Being (CPR, 123/5, 118).

Kant insists here that self-contentment cannot be called happiness or bliss. Self-contentment involves a negative satisfaction with a person's condition while happiness requires a positive participation of feeling, thus self-contentment cannot be called happiness. Also, self-contentment involves the awareness of a person's independence from and mastery of inclinations while bliss involves his or her complete independence from inclinations. Hence, self-contentment cannot be called bliss, though, Kant adds, it resembles bliss. According to this passage, self-contentment, happiness, and bliss are three separate and distinguishable states.

There are several ways that the claims in this passage may be connected with some of Kant's other claims about contentment, happiness, and bliss looked at earlier. First, the contentment whose source is satisfaction with one's own person has been described by various names, including self-contentment, intellectual contentment, and moral happiness. Kant defines the satisfaction that follows from the consciousness of virtue "self-contentment" and calls it an "intellectual contentment." Moral happiness has also been defined as contentment with one's own person and moral conduct. Thus, the terms self-contentment and moral happiness refer to the same state of affairs, that is, to a satisfaction whose source is moral, not sensible. Therefore, if, as Kant says in this passage, contentment with one's person cannot be called happiness, then neither can moral happiness.[18]

Second, Kant has made various claims about the relationship between self-contentment (moral happiness) and happiness, some of which are conflicting. This passage distinguishes self-contentment from happiness on grounds that it is a negative satisfaction and does not involve positive feelings. The source of self-contentment is moral while the source of happiness is sensible, gratified inclinations. In the former state, we are content with ourselves as rational, moral agents; in the latter, we are content with our condition as sensible beings. However, Kant has also indicated that self-contentment is a factor in happiness, that it is not a part of happiness, and that it is an analogue of happiness. Thus, while Kant makes some efforts to connect self-contentment and happiness, it is clear that self-contentment is not the same as happiness. They may be analogues, they may both involve a kind of contentment, but they are not descriptions of the same state.

Third, Kant suggests that there is a similarity between self-contentment and bliss. Self-contentment resembles bliss, he says, and his characterization of these two states suggests they are similar in that both involve independence from inclinations.[19] The difference is that the former is a partial independence from inclinations (the consciousness of a person's ability to master inclinations) and the latter is a complete independence from inclinations. There also seems to be a similarity between self-contentment and bliss in that Kant's accounts of both include the notion of an infinite progress.[20] Self-contentment or moral happiness is said to involve a disposition which ever progresses in goodness (Rel.61/6,67). Bliss is an idea which can only be contained in an unending progress (CPR,128n/5,123n). Both self-contentment and bliss have to do with a person's moral or intelligible nature and thus, the well-being that they refer to requires infinite progress towards the expression of independence from the sensible realm. Thus, self-contentment and bliss resemble one another but are not the same.

Finally, there is a relationship between bliss and happiness, although the passage at issue does not speak to it, and this relationship seems to be one of resemblance, not identity. Bliss is clearly like happiness in that it refers to a contentment, a well-being. But it is not the same as happiness because the cause of the contentment differs in the two cases as does the place where the contentment is realized. Bliss requires a consciousness of a person's independence from contingent causes; happiness does not. Bliss is attainable only in eternity; happiness is not.

In sum, Kant considers self-contentment or moral happiness to be an analogue of happiness. He states as well that self-contentment or moral happiness resembles bliss. On the basis of his texts, there is also a resemblance between bliss and happiness. The conclusion that follows is that while there are several types of contentment, there is only one type of happiness. There are various states of well-being; including happiness, self-contentment (so-called moral happiness), and bliss. All of these states involve some type of contentment and to that extent they resemble one another and are analogues.[21] But there are also differences among these states, the most noticeable being that happiness is a contentment with a person's sensible state while self-contentment (moral happiness) and bliss are contentments with a person's moral state. Thus, these three analogues of happiness involve a contentment with an intelligible cause. Happiness, as seen in section I, is a contentment that has a sensible cause, the satisfaction of inclinations. Since Kant gives an account of happiness as involving a sensible state of affairs (section I) and since his attempts to identify happiness with an intelligible or moral state of affairs are heavily qualified and often denied (section II), it follows that happiness concerns a person's condition in the sensible world. Happiness is not moral happiness, self-contentment, or bliss. Strictly speaking, moral happiness, self-contentment, and bliss ought not "stand under the name of" happiness nor should they "be called" happiness.

The last concern of this chapter is to consider how Kant's definition of happiness has implications for his doctrine of the highest good, which is treated in chapters 5 and 6. This chapter shows that Kant offers two accounts of happiness, one sensible and one intelligible, although the bulk of the evidence indicates he prefers the former account as a strict definition of happiness. In chapter 6, Kant talks of the highest good (in which happiness is a component) as both to be pursued "in" the world and as possible only "outside" the world.

There must be a connection between these two issues. On the one hand, perhaps the highest good is taken out of this world and thought in an intelligible world due to the nature of happiness. Kant says that bliss, under the name of happiness, cannot be reached in this world (CPR,133/5,129). He maintains that happiness cannot be realized on earth because our nature is never content (CJ,279-80/5,430). Perhaps the ambiguity in the highest good, the necessity of positing it in a future or intelligible world, can be blamed on happiness. Something about the nature or meaning of happiness leads to an ambiguity in the possible location of the highest good.

On the other hand, perhaps the relationship is the reverse. Kant's decision as to the location of the highest good might lead to an ambiguity in the meaning of happiness. His definitions of happiness tend to be descriptions of sensible states of satisfaction except in those passages in which he is considering happiness in proportion to worth, the highest good. Kant speaks of the necessity of positing the highest good in an intelligible world since the connection between virtue and happiness cannot be shown to be a necessary connection in the world of sense (CPR,119/5,115; A810-11,814/B838-39,842). In this way, the location of the highest good demands a certain sort of happiness. If the highest good is to be realized in the world, then happiness can be understood to be a sensible state, the satisfaction of sensible inclinations. However, if the highest good is to be realized out of the world, then this definition of happiness does not make sense. How can we speak of the satisfaction of our needs and inclinations in an intelligible world? In this case, a new definition of happiness is needed and so happiness in the intelligible world should perhaps be understood to be moral happiness, self-contentment, or bliss.

For the purposes of this study, it does not matter which ambiguity came first. My concern is neither to consider whether there is a causal connection between these two ideas nor to show which ambiguity came first in the mind or the writings of Kant.[22] What is clear is that the two issues are related. It is not by chance that there is ambiguity in the definition of happiness and ambiguity surrounding the location of the highest good. Happiness and the highest good are related problems since what happiness is affects and is affected by where the highest good is to be realized.

Chapter Two

The Negative Role of Happiness As Principle

Here, I focus on the negative claims Kant makes about happiness. I show that there is reason to argue that Kant does not consider happiness to be valuable in ethics. Those who see in Kant's ethic of duty a rejection of happiness are not so much wrong in what they say as they are in what they fail to say. It is true that Kant rejects happiness *as a principle* of ethics but it does not thereby follow that Kant rejects happiness in all of its roles. Here though, happiness will be considered only in its possible role as ground, motive, or principle of ethics. In this role, Kant states unequivocally, happiness is neither a good nor is its pursuit a duty.

Most of Kant's negative claims about happiness are to be found in the *Groundwork* and the Analytic section of the *Critique of Practical Reason*. There is good reason for this. These two works consider the possibility of a universal and necessary ethic. They represent Kant's search for the ground or the basis of ethics. He is not concerned here with the content or the matter of morality but with the possibility of a pure ethic. Hence, he says: "The sole aim of the present Groundwork is to seek out and establish *the supreme principle of morality*" (Gr.60/4,392). With regard to the second *Critique*, he claims: "Its task is merely to show that there is a pure practical reason" (CPR,3/5,3). So, the emphasis in these two works is on pure practical reason and the moral principle.

Therefore, these two works consider happiness largely (but not solely) from the perspective of pure practical reason and principles of morality. Kant argues that happiness is neither the object of a *pure* faculty of reason nor a *principle* of morality. So it is not surprising that Kant finds very little of value about happiness. But to reiterate, the fact that happiness fails to play a positive role when considering questions of the ground of pure practical reason and the principle of morality does not show that it has no positive role to play.

Before looking at Kant's discussion of principles and the possibility of a principle of happiness, consider how this chapter stands in relation to the chapters to follow. Much of what Kant has to say about ethics and about happiness is structured by his distinction between principles [*Principien*] and ends [*Zwecke*]. Put simply, Kant separates the principle of the action from the end, the object, of the action. The naive view is that Kant's ethic of principles *requires* the avoidance of ends. Ends, it is believed, have no place in an ethic of principles. The naive view presumes that principles and ends are mutually exclusive categories. This is not correct, as chapters 3, 4, 5, and 6 show.

However, the distinction between principles and ends is important to Kant, although it is by no means a distinction based on absolute difference or exclusivity. Principles and ends are two components of ethics, two ways of talking about moral actions. So while one component may be more important than the other given the asking of a certain question, Kant is not suggesting that ethics is possible with only one of the two components. He is not saying that an ethic of principles is an ethic without ends. Nor is he saying that if something fails to be a principle that it cannot be an end. The following reviews what he says about the will (*Wille*, in all cases) in order to show that there is no absolute exclusivity between principles and ends.

Kant refers to reason [*die Vernunft*] "as the faculty of principles [*das Vermögen der Principien*]" (CPR,124/5,119) and says that "the will [*den Willen*] could be defined as the faculty of ends [*das Vermögen der Zwecke*]" (CPR,61/5,58-59). What does this mean? Simply, the faculty of principles has as its task the providing of principles while the faculty of ends takes as its task the realizing of ends. The will (*den Willen*) is a faculty which can make an object real (CPR,62/5,60). A faculty is defined in terms of its task. Recall, for instance, in the first *Critique*, understanding is said to be the faculty of rules and reason is the faculty of principles (A299/B356). Reason as the faculty of principles provides the laws by means of which the rules of the understanding are unified (speculative reason) and the will is determined (practical reason). The will as the faculty of ends concerns the objects or matter whose pursuit is governed by the laws of reason.

Now if principles and ends are really mutually exclusive, then reason, the faculty of principles, and will, the faculty of ends, ought to be mutually exclusive faculties. But, obviously, this is not the case. Kant seems to find it difficult to speak of the will without also speaking of principles. In fact, in some sense, the will seems to be equivalent to practical reason and so the distinction between a faculty of ends and a faculty of principles breaks down.

For instance, Kant claims that only a rational being can act "in accordance with principles—and only so has he a *will* [*hat das Vermögen . . . nach Principien, zu handeln, oder einen Willen*]" (Gr.80/4,412). In other words, a will is equivalent to having the capacity to act in accordance with principles, that is, the power of determining oneself to action in accordance with the idea of certain laws (Gr.95/4,427). This makes it sound very much like the will is a faculty linked more closely with principles than with ends, as Kant stated above. This impression is reinforced by the following passage:

> a will [*einen Willen*], i.e., faculty of determining their [rational beings'] causality through the con-

> ception of a rule, and consequently in so far as they are competent to determine their actions according to principles and thus to act according to practical a priori principles (CPR,32/5,32).[1]

Kant characterizes the will as a faculty of acting according to principles. This implies that the will and practical reason may in fact be the same thing. Kant has said nothing about ends in these passages concerning the will so perhaps the will is actually practical reason. One passage from the *Groundwork* seems to confirm this: "the will [*der Wille*] is nothing but practical reason" (Gr.80/4,412).[2] So also in the second *Critique*: "reason . . . holds up the maxim of the will [*des Willens*] to the pure will [*den reinen Willen*], i.e., to itself regarded as a priori practical" (CPR,32/5,32).[3] It seems that the pure will is the same as pure practical reason.

Similarly, principles and the faculty of reason are not unrelated to ends and the faculty of the will. The *Groundwork* states that if there is to be a supreme practical principle, it must be that from the idea of something which is necessarily an end for everyone (an end in itself), it forms an objective principle of the will (Gr.96/4,428). Hence, principles are connected to, even dependent on, ends.

My interest is not in establishing whether the will or the pure will is in reality equivalent to pure practical reason. My concern is only with the way in which Kant's descriptions of the will come to sound more and more like his descriptions of practical reason, in spite of his distinction between them in terms of ends and principles. In other words, it is significant that regardless of his definition of the will as the faculty of ends, Kant more often speaks of the will in terms of principles and even as identical to the faculty of principles. These passages suggest that what can be spoken about in terms of ends can also be spoken about in terms of principles. A faculty of ends is also a faculty of principles. Presumably, the reverse is also true. A faculty of principles (reason) is also a faculty of ends (will). While laws and principles can be treated separately from objects and ends, the separation is only an abstraction. In fact, the principles of ethics (the form) are useless, without an application, apart from the ends or objects whose pursuit they direct. Similarly, the ends of ethics (the matter) are useless, unable to morally direct the will, apart from principles. This is perhaps analogous to the way in which concepts are empty without intuitions and intuitions are blind without concepts (A51/B75). The analogy is not perfect since concepts apply only to sensible objects while the ends of moral principles are not sensible objects. Still, both concepts and moral principles serve to determine: in the former case, the object is determined and knowledge results; in the latter case, the will is determined to action toward a certain end. In short, to speak of ethics in terms of principles does not entail the exclusion of ends. The distinction between principles and ends is not an opposition.

Let me turn then to Kant's treatment of happiness insofar as it relates to moral principles. The first section shows that the pursuit of happiness cannot be a moral principle, a pure principle, because it is directed toward an object, and it is an empirical principle. The second section considers the relationship between inclination and duty. The third section looks at Kant's distinction between legality and morality. The fourth section considers hypothetical and categorical imperatives. These sections lay out the various ways in which Kant excludes the concern for happiness from the realm of moral principles and so concludes that happiness if made a principle is neither a good nor is its pursuit a duty.

I. Pure Principles and Moral Value

Kant characterizes in several different ways the failure of happiness to be a principle of morality or to be the object of pure practical reason. Principles of happiness cannot be moral principles for the following reasons.

First, no principle which presupposes or depends on an object, end, or matter can be moral. Second, no principle which is empirical can be moral. Finally, principles of happiness always presuppose an object and they are empirical, and so they are never moral principles. Hence, Kant concludes, only pure (that is, nonempirical) principles that do not presuppose objects are moral principles and have moral value.

Kant claims that it is the principle which accords moral value to an action and not the object, end, or purpose of the action. The clearest statement of this is in the *Groundwork*.

> An action done from duty has its moral worth, *not in the purpose* to be attained by it, but in the maxim in accordance with which it is decided upon; it depends therefore, not on the realization of the object of the action, but solely on the *principle* of *volition* in accordance with which, irrespective of all objects of the faculty of desire, the action has been performed . . . [Moral worth] can be found nowhere but *in the principle of the will* [*im Princip des Willens*], irrespective of the ends [*der Zwecke*] which can be brought about by such an action (Gr.67-68/4,399-400).

Clearly, Kant wants to separate the principle or maxim of the will from the purpose, object, or end of the will. We must look to the principle on which the action is based to make a judgment of moral worth. Kant says again: "when moral value is in question, we are concerned, not with the actions which we see, but with their inner principles, which we cannot see" (Gr.75/4,407). In short, moral worth resides in and is bestowed by principles. Actions come to have moral worth because of the principles on which they are based and not because of any other component of the action.[4]

Now, not all principles are of moral worth. Although moral worth can be assigned only by principles, not all principles are capable of awarding moral worth. In particular, those principles that presuppose or are based on some other component of the action (the purpose, object, or end) cannot accord moral value. These principles themselves have no moral value. Kant says that practical laws (i.e., moral laws, principles of moral worth) "refer only to the will, irrespective of what is attained by its causality" (CPR,19/5,21). Similarly, principles "cannot yield any practical law . . . [when] it is not the form (accordance with law) but only the material which is decisive" (CPR,25/5,25).

Kant is specifying here a difference between principles which are moral and those which are not. A principle is moral when it is based not on the material but the form of the law. A principle is not moral when it presupposes or is based on its material content. He makes the point this way: "The sole principle of morality consists in independence from all material of the law (i.e., a desired object)" (CPR,33/5,33). And again: "it was shown that all material principles were wholly unfit to be the supreme moral law" (CPR,42/5,41).

In another way, Kant states that principles which are empirical are not of moral value. Kant believes that to connect a principle with anything "empirical" invalidates the worth of the principle. Thus, when a principle is associated with something empirical, it can no longer be a moral principle, it is not of moral value, and it cannot bestow moral worth on actions. Kant makes these points:

1. everything empirical added to them [moral concepts] is just so much taken away from their genuine influence and from the absolute value of the corresponding actions (Gr.79/4,411).
2. Hence everything that is empirical is, as a contribution to the principle of morality, not only wholly unsuitable for the purpose, but is even highly injurious to the purity of morals (Gr.93/4,426).
3. *Empirical principles* are always unfitted to serve as a ground for moral laws (Gr.109/4,442).

Thus, when a principle is empirical or when anything empirical is added to a principle, the moral worth of that principle is negated. For a principle to serve as a practical principle requires in part a freedom from anything empirical.[5]

Now there is a relationship between this point and the earlier one. Kant has said that moral principles are independent of objects and ends and that moral principles are independent of anything empirical. In one sense, these two claims seem to mean the same thing. In the second *Critique*, Kant says: "All practical principles which presuppose an object (material) of the faculty of desire as the determining ground of the will are without exception empirical and can furnish no practical laws" (CPR,19/5,21). This means that a principle is an empirical principle if it presupposes or is based on the object or material of the will. Later on Kant states, "a practical precept which presupposes a material and therefore empirical condition must never be reckoned a practical law" (CPR,34/5,34). This too suggests that a principle based on an object or material is thereby classified as an empirical principle. So to say that a moral principle must not be grounded on an object and that a moral principle must not be empirical is to say the same thing since a principle grounded on an object *is* an empirical principle. If all principles that presuppose an object are empirical then to report that moral principles do not presuppose an object is equivalent to reporting that moral principles are not empirical. And to say that moral principles are not empirical is equivalent to saying that they are not grounded on an object or end.

Unfortunately, Kant also makes claims that deny this equivalency. In the *Groundwork*, he classifies all the principles that seek the law "in the character of any of its objects" (Gr.108/4,441). The principles grounded on objects are of two types: empirical, rational (Gr.109/4,441-42). Similarly, in the second *Critique*, he lays out "all previous material principles of morality" (CPR,41/5,39). These material principles are principles grounded on objects and they are of two types: subjective (empirical), objective (based on reason) (CPR,41/5,40-41).

In both of these attempts to classify principles, Kant seems to be claiming that an empirical principle is not the same as a principle based on an object. There are other principles based on objects which are not empirical but rational. Thus, there is no identity between principles based on objects and empirical principles. The latter are an example of those principles based on objects.

Now with this qualification Kant's earlier claims may be amended. While it is not true that any principle that presupposes an object is an empirical principle, it still follows that any principle that presupposes an object fails to provide a moral law. Thus, it is not necessary to have an identity between principles grounded on objects and empirical principles in order to conclude that neither can be moral laws. Given that Kant recognizes that there are rational principles which are based on objects, he is not being redundant in claiming that moral principles neither are based on objects nor are they empirical. The former claim is simply a broader assertion.

By accepting Kant's classification of all material principles, the following conclusions result. First, a moral principle cannot be grounded on an object or end. Nonmoral principles, that is, those grounded on an object or end, can be either empirical or rational. Second, a moral principle cannot be empirical. Nonmoral principles on the other hand may be empirical though they need not be. Some are rational.

Now, what is the relevance of these conclusions to happiness, considered as a principle. The answer is simple. Kant's characterization of moral principles as principles not based on objects and as not empirical principles leads him to conclude that principles of happiness are not moral principles. Kant's conclusion is one with which all readers of the *Groundwork* and the second *Critique* are familiar. The principle of happiness is a principle based on the object or material of the will.[6] It is also an empirical principle. Principles based on the pursuit of happiness will never be moral and they contribute nothing to the realm of morality. It is from this conclusion that the negative role of happiness in Kant's ethics is apparent. Kant goes on to establish the connection between principles of happiness, principles based on objects, and empirical principles.

He says that "all the elements which belong to the concept of happiness are without exception empirical" (Gr.85/4,418) and that empirical principles are "drawn from the principle of *happiness*" (Gr.109/4,441-42). Happiness is an empirical concept and from a principle based on the pursuit of happiness follow all other empirical principles. This makes it sound as if all empirical principles are ultimately deducible from the principle of happiness or, in other words, that to be an empirical principle is more or less to be a principle of happiness.

Kant also sometimes speaks as if principles of happiness are more or less equivalent to empirical principles and even to material principles, that is, principles grounded on objects. It was shown above that there is reason to doubt Kant's claim that all principles grounded on objects are empirical principles. However, Kant uses this so-called identity between principles grounded on objects and empirical principles to argue that both are essentially the same as principles of happiness.

He comments in the second *Critique* on practical precepts which presuppose "a material and therefore empirical condition" (CPR,34/5,33-34). (This in spite of the earlier conclusion that not all material conditions are empirical.) He says that these precepts "all revolve about the principle of one's own happiness" (ibid.,34). He states later that "all determining grounds of the will [*des Willens*] (except the one and only pure practical law of reason, i.e., the moral law) are empirical and as such belong to the principle of happiness" (CPR,96/5,93). This claim asserts that any object which determines the will to act is empirical (contrary to the earlier conclusion that there are also rational objects which determine the will to act). All these empirical grounds are included under the principle of happiness. Finally Kant states: "All material practical principles are, as such, of one and the same kind and belong under the general principle of self-love or one's own happiness" (CPR,20/5,22). In other words, all material principles are versions of the principle of happiness.

Kant makes two claims here, both of which are overstated. First, he says that all principles that presuppose an object are principles of happiness. But what about principles based on the objects of moral feeling or perfection? Are they principles of happiness?[7] Second, he claims that all empirical principles are principles of happiness. Again, what about those empirical principles based on moral feeling? It is especially this so-called identity between empirical principles and the principle of happiness that Kant uses to show that the principle of happiness fails to be a moral principle. But there are reasons to be cautious in accepting the idea of an identity between empirical principles and principles of happiness.

The first reason is that there are difficulties with the language Kant uses to refer to the relationship between empirical principles and the principle of happiness. He says that empirical principles are "drawn from [*gebauet aus*]" the principle of happiness, that they "belong under [*gehören unter*]" the principle of happiness, that they "revolve about [*drehen sich insgesammt um*]" the principle of happiness, and that they "belong to [*gehören zum*]" the principle of happiness. It is reasonable to ask whether all of these terms posit the same sort of relationship. Is to "belong under" the same as to "belong to"? Does "revolving about" imply the same sense of dependency conveyed by belonging or drawing from?

The second reason is that there is further evidence that empirical principles and principles of happiness are not equivalent. In the *Groundwork*, Kant says that empirical principles are based "either on natural, or on moral, feeling" (Gr.109/4,441-42). He continues on to speak of the principle of personal happiness and a principle based on moral feeling as instances of empirical principles. In the second *Critique*, the list of principles identified as empirical includes four types: education, civil constitution, physical feeling (happiness), and moral feeling (CPR,41/5,40). Hence, when Kant systematically considers empirical principles, he finds principles in addition to the principle of happiness.

Clearly, Kant makes conflicting claims about the exact nature of the connection between empirical principles and the principle of happiness. He says all empirical principles belong to the principle of happiness and he says that the principle of happiness is one type of empirical principle. For the purposes of this study, it does not matter which of these is true. Both of these claims identify the principle of happiness as an empirical principle. It is this observation of the empirical nature of the principle of happiness that Kant uses to show that the principle of happiness fails to be moral.

There are several claims that this section has not attempted to make. First, it has reached no conclusion concerning the exact nature of the relationship between empirical principles and the principle of happiness. More important, no evaluation has been made regarding whether or not Kant is right about the nature of this relationship. Kant's claim that the principle of happiness is an empirical principle has been taken to be true in order to see what follows from this view concerning the role of happiness. Second, this section has not in any way considered Kant's proof that there is a pure moral principle and a pure practical reason. It is not necessary to this discussion of happiness to critique Kant's argument that there is a moral principle. What is crucial is to see the dichotomy Kant sets up between, on the one hand, principles based on ends, empirical principles, and the principle of happiness, and, on the other hand, principles not based on ends, pure principles, that is, moral principles. It is obvious from Kant's scheme that principles of happiness cannot be moral principles.

Therefore, Kant comes to exclude principles of happiness from the realm of morality since they fail to satisfy the requirements he sets for moral principles. These requirements are that a moral principle must not presuppose ends and it must not be empirical. Principles of happiness do both. Hence, Kant concludes that principles of happiness play no part and ought to be ignored in the realm of morality. He says that "principles for the pursuit of happiness cannot possibly produce morality" (CPR,123/5,119) and so "morals is not really the doctrine of how to make ourselves happy but of how we are to be *worthy* of happiness" (CPR,134/5,130). This explains one way in which Kant's discussion of happiness as a principle leads him to reject happiness from morality. The next section considers Kant's discussion of inclination and duty as another way of showing that principles of happiness fall outside morality.

II. Inclination versus Duty

Kant separates principles of happiness from moral principles. Indeed he maintains that the differentiation between "the doctrine of happiness" and "the doctrine of morality" is "the first and most important task charged to the Analytic of Pure Practical Reason" (CPR,95/5,92). Now there are other ways in which Kant speaks of this distinction between principles of happiness and moral principles. One is the distinction between inclination and duty.

In a passage similar to the one above regarding the distinction between the doctrines of happiness and morality, Kant comments on how "distinct and sharp are the boundaries between morality and self-love" (CPR,37/5,36). He says later that "everything in self-love belongs to inclination" (CPR,77/5,74). Kant is here distinguishing morality, on the one hand, from happiness, self-love, and inclination, on the other hand.

Kant also links the inclinations to empiricism in a way reminiscent of his linking of principles of happiness to empirical principles. He says that "empiricism is allied with the inclinations" (CPR,74/5,71) and that it substitutes an empirical interest for duty. Thus, the inclinations are said to be tied to the empirical. A principle grounded on inclinations or self-love is therefore an empirical principle and that is precisely how principles of happiness are characterized. Consequently, when Kant speaks of maxims of inclination or actions based on inclination, he can be understood to be speaking about principles of happiness or actions based on the desire for happiness. Kant says this when he identifies that "powerful counterweight to all the commands of duty" as "the counterweight of his [a person's] needs and inclinations, whose total satisfaction he grasps under the name of 'happiness'" (Gr.73/4,405). Hence, to distinguish duty from inclination is one way to distinguish morality from happiness.

This conclusion is further confirmed by several comments Kant makes about moral worth. He claims that if a person acts "not from inclination or fear but from duty; then indeed his maxim has a moral content" (Gr.66/4,398). Again, he maintains, "neither fear nor inclination . . . is the motive which can give an action moral worth" (Gr.107/4,440). In other words, a maxim based on inclination has no moral content and can accord no moral worth to actions. This is exactly what Kant said about the principle of happiness in the last section. Thus, when Kant speaks of duty versus inclination, he is speaking as well about moral principles versus principles of happiness.

Kant first sets up the contrast between duty and inclination by speaking of a "counterweight" (in a passage quoted above) and a "natural dialectic." The whole passage reads:

> Man feels in himself a powerful counterweight to all the commands of duty presented to him by reason as so worthy of esteem—the counterweight of his needs and inclinations, whose total satis-

> faction he grasps under the name of 'happiness.' But reason, without promising anything to inclination, enjoins its commands relentlessly, and therefore, so to speak, with disregard and neglect of these turbulent and seemingly equitable claims (which refuse to be suppressed by any command). From this there arises a *natural dialectic*—that is, a disposition to quibble with these strict laws of duty, to throw doubt on their validity or at least on their purity and strictness, and to make them, where possible, more adapted to our wishes and inclinations (Gr.73/4,405).

Thus, standing counter to the commands of duty are the demands of inclination, of happiness. Human beings discover two sides to themselves, both claiming to offer a principle for governing conduct. Reason offers the commands of duty, inclination offers the demands of happiness.[8] This juxtaposition results in a natural dialectic or contrast between the claims of duty and those of inclination. Kant later speaks of this dialectic as one of "antagonistic claims" and "ambiguity" (ibid.).

What is interesting is the exact nature of this dialectic. That there is a differentiation or boundary between the claims of duty and those of inclination is clear from what has gone before. There remains the question as to the nature of this dialectic.

Kant characterizes the boundary between morality and inclination in two different ways. The first describes the relationship between duty and inclination as one of independence from each other. The second describes the relationship as one of conflict. It may be that both these descriptions apply. The claims of duty and those of inclination are both independent from and in conflict with each other. But the two descriptions clearly differ. To be "independent from" is not necessarily to be "in conflict with." Also, it makes a difference to Kant's account of the place of happiness in ethics if a maxim based on happiness is only independent of a moral maxim or if it conflicts with a moral maxim. Kant would be likely to be more negative about the claims of happiness if they actually conflict with duty than if they are simply independent of duty. Put this way, if the demand for happiness is separate from moral commands, it is of negative value because it has nothing to do with morality. But if it is in conflict with moral commands, then it is of negative value because it opposes, contradicts, holds human beings back from, morality. In the latter case, maxims of happiness are a greater threat to duty and so the claims of happiness have to be rejected more emphatically than they would in the former case.

The first way of characterizing the relationship between inclination and duty is that of independence. Kant often speaks as if duty and inclination have nothing to do with each other, that is, as if they are so separate from each other that they do not affect or pertain to each other. For instance, he says that an action done from duty "has to set aside altogether the influence of inclination" (Gr.68/4,400). He insists that duty "is in no way based on feelings, impulses, and inclinations" (Gr.102/4,434). Reason, he says, offers the commands of duty "with disregard and neglect" of the claims of inclination (Gr.73/4,405). All these passages refer to a separation between the claims of duty and the claims of inclination but do not mention any hostility between them.

There are other indications of the independence of moral claims from the claims of inclination. Kant states that reason must determine the will "not in the service of the inclinations" (CPR,24/5,25). Reason, he says, exhibits the moral law as "completely independent of [*unabhängigen*] and not to be outweighed by any sensuous condition" (CPR,29/5,30). Reason holds up the maxim of the will "regardless of what inclination may say to the contrary" (CPR,32/5,32). That which belongs to the principle of happiness "must be separated from the supreme practical principle and never be incorporated with it as a condition" (CPR,96-97/5,93). Finally, "maxims of virtue and those of one's own happiness are wholly heterogeneous" (CPR,117/5,112).

What is common to all these passages is the idea that the commands of duty and the demands of inclination are independent of and need not impinge on each other. Maxims based on inclination and happiness are of no value in ethics precisely because they lie outside of, and can be ignored by, maxims based on duty, and hence morality.

The second way Kant characterizes the relationship between duty and inclination is that of conflict. Kant refers to the antagonistic claims of reason's principle and the maxims of inclination (Gr.73/4,405) and to an "opposition [*Widerstand*] of inclination to the precept of reason (*antagonismus*)" (Gr.92/4,424). The moral law, he says, is "in conflict with [*im Gegensatze mit*] its subjective antagonists (our inclinations)" (CPR,76/5,73). Kant mentions later "the conflict [*des Streits*] which now the moral disposition has to wage with inclinations" (CPR,152/5,147).

These passages suggest that the demands of inclination are not simply separate from the principle of duty but that they oppose it. It is not just a neutral separation Kant is talking about now but an antagonism. Thus, the moral principle cannot simply ignore the inclinations or happiness, it must work against them. Indeed, there are places where Kant speaks of the activity of the moral law in opposing inclination. He states that the moral law "blocks the inclinations" (CPR,77/5,74), it acts "by thwarting all our inclinations" (CPR,75/5,73), and thus, there is "the resistance [*Widerstrebung*] of a practically legislating reason to all interfering inclinations" (CPR,95/5,92).

Conversely, inclination also works against the moral principle. The inclinations "secretly work against [*entgegen wirken*] it [the moral law]" (CPR,89/5,86), and incentives of happiness "are a hindrance to the influence of the moral law on the human heart" (CPR,160/5,156). These claims imply that the relationship between duty and inclination is not simply one of benign neglect. They are more than independent of one another, they oppose, conflict, and work against each other.

Two other works confirm Kant's tendency to speak in diverse ways about the relationship between duty and inclination. In the *Lectures on Ethics*, Kant states that morality is "independent of [*unabhängig von*] all inclination" and that it cannot "be based on the subjective laws of men's inclinations" (LE,38/M,47). But he also claims that: "Ethics is no analysis of inclination but a prescription which is contrary to all inclination [*wider alle Neigung ist*]" (LE,37/M,45). Again, Kant's descriptions speak of independence and of contrariness. The same point is made in the *Metaphysics of Morals*. There Kant maintains that the laws of morality "command everyone without regard to his inclinations" (MM,15/6,216). But he states that when human beings obey the moral law, they do so "in conflict with their inclinations [*mit Widerstand ihrer Neigung*]" (MM,36/6,379). There is, thus, this additional evidence that Kant considers the commands of morality and the demands of inclination to be both independent of each other and in conflict with each other.

Now, what are we to make of these texts and Kant's discussion of independence and conflict? Either Kant is just not very careful about the way he describes the relationship of duty and inclination or perhaps he is speaking in one way when he refers to their independence and in another way when he asserts their conflict. Returning to the texts, there seem to be three possible ways of arguing for the latter point, namely, that the sense in which there is independence is different from the sense in which there is conflict.

First, it appears that when Kant discusses the independence of duty and inclination, he speaks generally about maxims of duty and inclination, and about the claims of reason versus those of inclination, although when he considers the conflict between duty and inclination, he speaks more specifically of the moral law, the principle of reason versus inclination. Perhaps the independence of duty and inclination is at the level of maxims and claims and their conflict is at the level of principles and laws. For instance, the first *Critique* states that when regulative principles of speculative reason are employed as constitutive, objective principles, they may come into conflict with each other although when treated merely as maxims, there is no real conflict [*kein wahrer Widerstreit*] (A666/B694).

But, while it is tempting to try to resolve the issue this way, there is evidence that works against it. It is not always true that when speaking of independence the language is that of maxims. In several of the passages where Kant identifies the independence of duty from inclination, he uses the language of principles and laws (CPR,29/5,30; CPR,96-97/5,93; MM,15/6,216). For instance, in the second *Critique*, Kant says: "this distinction of the principle of happiness from that of morality is not for this reason an opposition [*Entgegensetzung*] between them" (CPR,96/5,93). The moral principle simply takes no account of (ignores, is independent from) principles of happiness. It seems to be more true that when speaking of conflict the language is that of principles although in the passages cited both the moral disposition and ethics are also said to be in conflict with inclination. Thus, perhaps the distinction between maxims and principles could be used to resolve the question of independence versus conflict but it is evident that Kant does not strictly align maxims with independence and principles with conflict.

Second, the *Metaphysics of Morals* raises the possibility that the laws of duty are independent of inclination but the obeying of these laws (the act of obedience) conflicts with inclination. This seems to mean that the law of duty is not in itself contrary to inclination but that the practice of the law does end up being so contrary. Apparently, the transition from the intelligible world (where the moral law is given) to the sensible world (where the moral law is put into effect) leads the relationship of independence into one of conflict. But this view, that the obeying of the moral law runs counter to inclination, is challenged by other texts. For instance, Kant says that although people have the greatest inclination not to kill themselves, only when they preserve themselves out of duty does the act of self-preservation have moral worth (Gr.65-66/4,397-98). Hence, an act that is done for the sake of the moral law need not conflict with inclination. It seems unlikely that the act of obeying the moral law accounts for the conflict between duty and inclination, especially given the other texts in which it is the moral law which conflicts with inclination.

The third possibility is more intriguing. In the passages cited, Kant never suggests that there is a conflict between the principle of happiness and the moral principle. In fact, he denies that any such conflict exists (CPR,96-97/5,93). He insists that the principle of happiness must be kept separate from the supreme practical principle so that the moral principle takes no account of it, but there is no opposition between them. The conflict that exists is between inclination and duty or even inclination and the moral disposition but not between the principle of happiness and the moral law. In this case, there is no inconsistency in Kant's talk of independence and conflict given that he is not referring to the same relationship in both cases. There is also good news on the question of happiness, according to this view. While inclination may conflict with and work against the moral law, principles of happiness do not. Thus, although principles of happiness have nothing to do with morality, they do not by nature contradict morality. A principle of happiness is a threat to morality but not the antithesis of morality.

One problem with this account is that it depends on a distinction between, on the one hand, inclination and inclinations, and, on the other hand, a principle of happiness. Kant defines happiness as the satisfaction of one's inclinations and he distinguishes morality from happiness and from self-love which "belongs to" inclination. Thus, while much of what Kant says about inclination and its separation from morality seems to apply as well to happiness, it appears that a principle of happiness when looked at alone stands in a relationship to morality unlike that of inclination generally. While inclination is both independent from and in conflict with duty, a principle of happiness is only independent from it. This is due perhaps to Kant's claim that one end all finite rational beings share is that of happiness (while inclination may vary person to person, the end of happiness does not). A principle based on happiness is at least a universal and necessary principle, even though conditioned by the end of happiness. Perhaps it is also due in part to Kant's recognition of the importance of happiness to morality. Certainly as Kant goes on to speak of indirect duties to pursue personal happiness and happiness as a part of the highest good, it is clear that happiness is not in conflict with morality and perhaps neither is a principle of happiness, although inclination generally does so conflict.

Thus, there are several approaches that might be taken to Kant's discussion of inclination and duty. Kant is not especially careful in defining the nature of their relationship, except minimally, they exclude each other. He is also not especially exact in laying out the relationship between inclination and principles of happiness. While inclination may conflict with duty, principles of happiness, it seems, do not. What is clear is that the contrast between inclination and duty provides Kant with one way of explicating the independence of morality from inclination and principles of happiness.

III. Legality versus Morality

A third way in which happiness is excluded from ethics in its role as principle is revealed in Kant's distinction between legality and morality. Kant uses the terms "legality" and "morality" to distinguish between two possible incentives of the will. Legality and morality are ways of classifying a will's incentive and of judging the moral worth of the will's resulting action. Kant's discussion of incentives and moral worth in terms of the legality/morality distinction provides another way of explaining why a principle of happiness is not moral.

Kant distinguishes between acts which *conform to* the moral law and those which are done *for the sake of* the moral law. He says: "For if any action is to be morally good, it is not enough that it should *conform* to the moral law [*es dem sittlichen Gesetze gemäss sei*]—it must also be done *for the sake of the moral law* [*es muss auch um desselben willen geschehen*]" (Gr.57-58/4,390). He allows thus that some actions are done "*in conformity with duty* [*pflichtmässig*], but not *from the motive of duty* [*aus Pflicht*]" (Gr.65/4,398). Kant's concern is that actions which simply conform to the moral law do so contingently, accidentally, and not because they were done out of duty. An action may look like a moral action but not be motivated by the moral principle. This conformity or resemblance is not enough to make the action morally good in the absence of the moral principle or motive.

In the second *Critique*, Kant uses similar terms to make this distinction and he uses the language of legality and morality to describe this distinction. He says we can distinguish between having acted "*according to duty* [*pflichtmässig*] and *from duty* [*aus Pflicht*], i.e., from respect for the law. The former, legality, is possible even if inclinations alone are the determining grounds of the will, but the latter, morality or moral worth, can be conceded only where the action occurs from duty, i.e., merely for the sake of the law [*blos um des Gesetzes willen*]" (CPR,84/5,81). Thus, an action which is done from duty is moral because the incentive or motive of the action is the moral law. An action which accords with duty is only legal since its incentive is not the moral law. Clearly, the distinction between acting from duty and acting according to duty is a way of talking about a difference between the principles of actions. Kant puts it this way in the *Metaphysics of Morals*: "The agreement of an action with the law of duty is its legality (*legalitas*); that of the maxim of the action with the law is its morality (*moralitas*)" (MM,25/6,225). To be legal, it is enough that the action agree with duty (whatever the principle of the action may be). To be moral, the principle of the action must agree with duty, that is, the principle of the action must be the moral law.

Kant offers these other descriptions of the difference between legality and morality.

1. If the determination of the will occurs in accordance with the moral law but only by means of a feeling . . . and if the action thus occurs not for the sake of the law [*nicht um des Gesetzes willen*], it has legality but not morality (CPR,74/5,71).

2. the direct thought of the law and objective obedience to it as duty . . . must be thought of as the real incentives of actions, for otherwise legality of actions but not morality of intentions would result (CPR,155/5,151).

3. everything must be directed to the thought of the law as the determining ground if the action is not to contain mere legality but also morality (CPR,122/5,118).

Kant's point is simple. If the determining ground of the will is duty, then the resulting action is moral. This is equivalent to saying that the principle of the action must be the moral law if the action is to be moral. If, on the other hand, the determining ground or principle of the action is not the moral law, then the action can at best be legal. While a legal action outwardly resembles a moral action, it does not inwardly resemble a moral action since its principle is not the moral law. It is a difference in principles that separates legal from moral actions. The distinction between morality and legality is a further way of talking about Kant's earlier distinctions between moral and nonmoral principles, and between duty and inclination.

There are really three possible states of affairs if attention is paid to the principle of the action and the resulting action. First, the principle of the act may be the moral law in which case the resulting action will be moral. Second, the principle of the act may not be the moral law (it may be a feeling, an inclination, i.e., any nonmoral principle) although the resulting action is the same as the action that results from the moral principle (i.e., the action conforms to duty). In this case, the action is legal but not moral. Third, the principle of the act may not be the moral law and the resulting action may be different from the action that results from the moral principle. In this case, the action is neither moral nor legal. Hence, Kant uses the terms legality and morality to distinguish apparently identical actions in terms of the different principles which ground them.

There is one other slightly different description Kant gives of legality and morality. Kant talks about a situation in which the moral law is followed for the sake of a person's own advantage. He concludes: "The letter of the law (legality) would be met with in our actions, but the spirit of the law (morality) would not be found in our intentions" (CPR,156/5,152). Here Kant suggests that legality is carrying out the letter of the law while morality is the accomplishing of the spirit of the law. An action is legal if it follows the letter of the law (does what the law says to do). An action is moral if it obeys the spirit of the law (does what the law says to do because the law says to do it, that is, for the reason the law gives for doing it).

Now, since the legality/morality distinction is essentially a point about the principles of actions, it is not hard to connect it with the discussion of the principle of happiness. Put briefly, in drawing a distinction between legality and morality Kant is making a point, a negative point, about the principle of happiness. If something other than the moral law motivates an action, the action is at best legal. It follows quite obviously that happiness taken as a principle or as the determining ground of the will can never produce a moral act but at best a legal act.

Morality cannot result from principles of happiness.

There are three passages in which Kant implies a conclusion like this concerning the relation of happiness to legality though he does not anywhere use the term happiness. The first place is in the *Groundwork*. There Kant gives an example to illustrate the difference between an act in conformity with duty and an act done from duty. He says that most people preserve their lives in conformity with duty but because it serves their inclination to do so. This action is a legal action but not a moral action since it is not grounded on duty, but inclination (Gr.65/4,397-98). On the contrary, when a person has no inclination to preserve his or her life but preserves it anyway from the motive of duty, then the act is moral. Thus, two people may have done the same thing, preserved their lives, but the first has done so out of inclination (legality) while the second has done so out of duty (morality). The motive contrasted with duty is inclination. Kant's characterization of a moral act is an act based on duty while a legal act is an act based on inclination that resembles the act done from duty. Legality occurs where the motive of the act is inclination. Since happiness is the satisfaction of inclinations and principles of happiness are conditioned by the end of happiness, which all human beings share and toward which they have the strongest and deepest inclination (Gr.67/4,399), it follows that when the principle of happiness motivates an act, the resulting act is never moral, but, at best, legal. Acts motivated by inclination are not moral; acts motivated by happiness are not moral.

The same connection between legality and happiness is suggested in the second *Critique*. Kant says that "legality, is possible even if inclinations alone are the determining grounds of the will" (CPR,84/5,81). Even if inclination alone is motivating the will, legality is possible. Legality allows for motives of inclination and happiness while morality does not. Again, Kant is saying that happiness considered in its role as principle can accomplish only legal actions, not moral actions.

Finally, in the *Metaphysics of Morals*, Kant connects morality with the law and legality with the end. This connection has the effect of linking principles of happiness and legality. Kant distinguishes between the law taken as an incentive on which morality rests and the end taken as an incentive on which legality rests (MM,57/6,398). The claim is that the incentive or principle of the moral act is the law while the incentive or principle of the legal act is the end. This is reminiscent of a conclusion from section I, that is, no principle grounded on an end can be moral. Empirical principles and principles of happiness are based on ends or objects and hence, they fail to be moral principles. Kant's talk about legality in contrast to morality provides one more way for him to describe the failure of principles of happiness to be moral principles.

IV. Hypothetical Imperatives versus Categorical Imperatives

Kant takes one other approach in his attempt to show how principles of happiness fail to be moral. His distinction between hypothetical imperatives (one example of which is pragmatic principles, that is, principles of prudence) and categorical imperatives reveals the failure of happiness to be a moral principle. He also uses the terms heteronomy and autonomy to point to the difference between principles of happiness and moral principles.

Granted not all of the above contrasts are perfectly identical. For instance, the term "imperative" conveys something more than the previously employed term "principle" (Gr.80-81/4,413). Yet, from the perspective of happiness understood as a principle for action, the point of these distinctions is the same. A principle of happiness is said to be an empirical principle, grounded in inclination, not duty, resulting in legality, not morality, an example of a hypothetical imperative, not a moral law, and thus an example of heteronomy, not autonomy. Let me consider how principles of happiness come to be classified as hypothetical imperatives and as examples of heteronomy and so are condemned on those grounds.

Imperatives are either categorical or hypothetical (Gr.82/4,414). Categorical imperatives are concerned "not with the matter of the action" (Gr.84/4,416). They are called imperatives of morality. The commands of a categorical imperative "must be followed even against inclination" (ibid.). Hypothetical imperatives, on the other hand, determine a will "in respect to its effect and its sufficiency to bring this effect about" (CPR,18/5,20). Hypothetical imperatives thus concern the matter of the action.[9] They can be of two sorts; either technical imperatives of skill (concerned with possible ends) or pragmatic imperatives of prudence (concerned with actual ends, for instance, happiness). All imperatives aimed at the end of happiness are hypothetical imperatives. Kant says, "an imperative concerned with the choice of means to one's own happiness . . . remains *hypothetical*" (Gr.83/4,416).

The principle of happiness is here characterized in ways that are familiar. A principle of happiness is concerned with the effect of the will or the matter of the action. Principles of happiness are hypothetical imperatives and so distinguished from categorical imperatives which neither are based on the matter of the action nor take into account inclination.

Hypothetical imperatives appear as rules of skill or as counsels of prudence while categorical imperatives appear as laws of morality (Gr.84/4,416-17). If duties depend on the relation of the action to the ends of happiness, then "they would depend on our inclinations and so be governed by rules of prudence" (LE,120-21/M,150). Rules of prudence, that is, one type of hypothetical imperative, aim to determine a will concerned with inclination and the ends of happiness. Thus, whatever is said about the moral value of hypothetical imperatives will apply as well to principles of happiness, which are the most visible examples of hypothetical imperatives.

Kant establishes a clear differentiation between morality and prudence or between principles of morality and principles of prudence. He states that "the pragmatic principle is dependent on the inclinations. Morality is, however, independent of all inclination, and it is not, therefore, grounded in any pragmatic principle" (LE,38/M,46-47). Practical philosophy, he maintains, includes only rules of prudence and rules of morality (LE,4/M,5). With respect to the former, practical philosophy is pragmatic; with respect to the latter, it is ethical. Prudence is "the ability to use the means towards the universal end of man, that is, happiness" (ibid.). However, the commands of "moral imperatives are absolute and regardless of the end" (LE,5/M,6).

The contrast is absolute. On the one hand, there are principles of prudence, which are hypothetical imperatives, depend on the inclinations, and are directed towards the end of happiness. On the other hand, there are principles of morality, categorical imperatives, which do not depend on the inclinations, ends, or happiness. Happiness is identified as the concern of pragmatic principles. Kant summarizes these points in this passage:

> The practical law, derived from the motive of *happiness*, I term pragmatic (rule of prudence), and that law, if there is such a law, which has no other motive than *worthiness of being happy*, I term moral (law of morality). . . . The former is based on empirical principles . . . This latter law can therefore be based on mere ideas of pure reason, and known *a priori* (A806/B834).

Finally, Kant connects these claims about hypothetical and categorical imperatives, principles of prudence and principles of morality, with his notions of heteronomy and autonomy. He defines autonomy in these ways:

> Autonomy of the will is the property the will has of being a law to itself (independently of every property belonging to the objects of volition) (Gr.108/4,440).

> The *autonomy* of the will is the sole principle of all moral laws and of the duties conforming to them (CPR,33/5,33).

He goes on to claim that "the above principle of autonomy is the sole principle of ethics" (Gr.108/4,440). The principle of morality must be a categorical imperative and as such it commands precisely this autonomy (ibid.). Thus, the moral law "expresses nothing else than the autonomy of the pure practical reason" (CPR,33-34/5,33). Therefore, autonomy is simply the will's ascribing of the moral law, that is, the categorical imperative, to itself.

Heteronomy, on the other hand, occurs when the will in choosing a principle is motivated "from a certain interest" (Gr.100/4,433). Heteronomy results when the will seeks the moral law "in the character of any of its objects" (Gr.108/4,441). In this case, it is the object which gives the will the law and this relation, says Kant, "can give rise only to hypothetical imperatives" (ibid.). Heteronomy is said to be opposed to "the principle of duty and to the morality of the will" (CPR,33/5,33). Kant claims that if an object of a desire "comes into the practical law *as a condition of its possibility*, there results heteronomy of choice, or dependence on natural laws in following some impulse or inclination" (CPR,34/5,33). Thus, he summarizes: "Wherever an object of the will has to be put down as the basis for prescribing a rule to determine the will, there the rule is heteronomy; . . . consequently it can never give a moral—that is, a categorical—command" (Gr.111/4,444).

Again, the connection is a simple one. "Autonomy" and "heteronomy" are descriptions of principles or rules. They are also properties of the will that formulates these principles or rules. Insofar as autonomy and heteronomy are principles, they refer respectively to principles generated by the will and principles generated by the will's object. The former principles are conditionless, that is, categorical, while the latter principles are conditioned, that is, hypothetical. Consequently, principles of autonomy are moral and principles of heteronomy are not moral.

Since the identification between autonomy and categorical principles and between heteronomy and hypothetical principles is so straightforward, it is easy to see how autonomy and heteronomy relate to happiness. Since principles of happiness have already been identified as examples of hypothetical imperatives, and heteronomy gives rise only to hypothetical imperatives, obviously, principles of happiness are heteronomous. Although Kant does not use the term "happiness" in his description of heteronomy, there are indications of its presence. Kant defines heteronomy as acting from an interest, motivated by an object of desire, and the following of an impulse or inclination. Principles of happiness are also grounded on the desire for some object of inclination and as such are good examples of heteronomous principles. In sum, the autonomy/heteronomy distinction reflects the categorical/hypothetical distinction and so both make similar points about the role of principles of happiness. The language of autonomy/heteronomy gives Kant a further way of characterizing the failure of certain principles, especially principles of happiness, to be moral.

For Kant, principles of happiness fail to be moral because they are principles based on objects or ends and because they are empirical principles. Principles of happiness are based on inclination and therefore they are by definition excluded from the arena of morality. Kant talks about principles of happiness as resulting in legality, not morality. He classifies them as rules of prudence, as examples of hypothetical imperatives, and as instances of heteronomy. While principles of happiness may not be the *only* examples of empirical principles, they are the most visible examples. Because the principle of happiness is the one principle grounded on an end that is shared by all human beings, Kant's attempt to rid morality of principles that are not moral often operates as an attempt to rid morality of the principle of happiness. His point however is unambiguous. Happiness considered in its role as a principle of ethics is not of moral value (is not good) and its pursuit is not a duty.

Chapter Three

The Positive Role of Happiness As Natural End

The previous chapter considered the way Kant distinguishes principles from ends and how the issue of happiness relates to principles. Happiness as a principle, as an example of a hypothetical imperative, plays only a negative role in Kant's account of ethics. Now I turn to Kant's discussion of ends. This amounts to a shift away from the formal aspect of a maxim or law toward its material aspect, that is, its content.

In this chapter, the focus will be on Kant's treatment of happiness as a natural end and the extent to which this treatment entails a positive role for happiness in ethics. Section I reviews the way Kant defines ends. Section II considers Kant's claims about the place of ends in a moral theory. In particular, the problem of whether or not Kant is consistent in describing ends as determining grounds of the will is addressed. The question is whether ends must dictate principles or whether they need not dictate principles. Section III considers happiness as a natural end and insofar as it is a natural end, a good. I look also at Kant's caution that although happiness as a natural end is good, its pursuit is not thereby a duty.

I. Definition of End

Kant is straightforward in defining what he means by "end." He speaks of "an end [*Zweck*] as the material of the will [*die Materie des Willens*]" (CPR,42/5,41). He claims that: "The material of a practical principle is the object of the will [*Die Materie eines praktischen Princips ist der Gegenstand des Willens*]" (CPR,26/5,27). Often in the Dialectic section of the second *Critique* when Kant is speaking of the highest good, he identifies the highest good as both object and end of the will. He claims: "The highest good is the necessary highest end [*Zweck*] of a morally determined will and a true object [*Object*] thereof" (CPR,119/5,115). He refers to "the concept of the highest good as the object and final end [*das Object und den Endzweck*] of pure practical reason" (CPR,134/5,129). Thus, Kant appears to be calling an end that which is the material or the object of the will.

In the *Groundwork*, there seems to be an identification of end, matter, and object of the will. Kant refers to "matter-that is, an end [*Materie, nämlich einen Zweck*]" (Gr.104/4,436). Hence, an end is the material of the maxim, of the will. Kant says that reason cannot explain how it is that pure reason can be practical; that is, how a bare principle can supply a motive to reason "without any matter (or object) of the will [*ohne alle Materie (Gegenstand) des Willens*] in which we could take some antecedent interest" (Gr.129/4,461). The *Metaphysics of Morals* confirms that: "the end is the matter (object) of choice [*der Zweck die Materie (Object) der Willkür ist*]" (MM,54/6,395). In sum, the evidence indicates that Kant is using the terms *Zweck*, *Materie*, *Object*, and *Gegenstand* (end, matter, and object) to refer to the same thing.[1]

There is one other point worth noting in the above passages. In the *Metaphysics of Morals*, Kant speaks of ends as objects of *Willkür* unlike the other texts which describe them as objects of *Wille*. He identifies an end with "the matter of choice [*Willkür*]" (MM,37/6,380), "an object of choice [*Willkür*]" (MM,38/6,381), and "an object of free choice [*Willkür*]" (MM,42/6,384). But Kant does not adopt this language exclusively, for he also claims that an end is "the matter of the will [*Willens*]"

(MM,33/6,376). What effect does this additional description have on the definition of ends?

The effect of the *Wille/Willkür* distinction on the definition of ends is inconsequential. Kant's view is this. The matter of *Willkür* may be contrary to duty so pure practical reason proposes its own opposing end, that is, ends which are at the same time duties. Pure practical reason commands a priori ends which are at the same time duties. Morality concerns the objects of *Willkür* under its own laws (MM,43/6,385), that is, under the laws of freedom. *Willkür* is dictated to by *Wille* so that in the realm of morality, the ends of *Wille* are the ends of *Willkür*. What is chosen is what is dictated by reason, what is self-legislated. Kant points out that the concept of duty is the concept of a "constraint of free choice [*Willkür*] by law [*Gesetz*]" (MM,36/6,379). *Willkür* is subject to the constraint of the law of pure practical reason which puts forward certain ends as required ends. This constraint Kant describes as self-constraint according to a principle of internal freedom (MM,53/6,394). Hence, while the ends of free choice may in general be more varied than the ends of pure practical reason, in the realm of morality, these ends are the same because the moral law of pure reason constrains the faculty of free choice to adopt its ends. Ends are the objects of *Willkür* and *Wille* and in the case of an act of moral willing both faculties have the same end.

Apart from this identification of end with matter and object, there are several places where Kant links the notion of end with that of inclination. He says:

> Now an action done from duty has to set aside altogether the influence of inclination [*den Einfluss der Neigung*], and along with inclination every object of the will [*jeden Gegenstand des Willens*] (Gr.68/4,400).

> An *end* [*Zweck*] is always the object of an *inclination* [*der Gegenstand einer Zuneigung*], that is, of an immediate craving for possession of a thing through one's action (Rel.6n/6,6).

This linking of end with inclination has two major effects. First, it connects the notion of end with the idea of happiness. As chapter 1 showed, happiness involves a satisfaction of one's inclinations. When Kant speaks of needs and inclinations, he generally means happiness.[2] Second, it suggests that ends since tied to inclination and hence to happiness probably must be removed from or set aside from a categorical ethic. A categorical ethic, an ethic which is of moral value, is based on a principle which is not derived from inclinations or happiness. Insofar as ends are tied to inclinations and serve to ground principles, these ends and the principles they ground will be of no positive moral value in a categorical ethic.

In other words, this linking of ends and inclination leads to a consideration of the role of ends. The possibilities are these. Either ends are necessarily tied to inclinations and happiness or they are not. If they are, then there are two choices. Either Kant has nothing else to say about ends apart from denouncing the way they and inclinations and happiness initiate principles, or Kant has more to say about ends since they and inclinations and happiness can function in ways quite apart from their role in initiating principles. Finally, if ends are not necessarily tied to inclinations and happiness, then it is important to look specifically at what Kant says about the role of ends apart from the question of inclinations and happiness.

My claim is that even if ends are necessarily tied to inclinations and happiness, it does not follow that they are of no value in ethics. There may be value to ends, inclinations, and happiness even if they ought not serve to ground moral principles. But since in fact, ends need not be tied to inclinations and happiness, it is possible for some ends to play a positive role in Kant's ethic in a way not possible to ends of inclination or happiness. Let me turn next to a consideration of the place of ends in Kant's moral theory.

II. Place of Ends

I begin with Kant's simplest comments on the role of ends and conclude with a consideration of some problems in his account. Kant is clearest when he states that ethics entails talk about ends. His ethic is not possible and, in fact, he believes that no ethic is possible that fails to treat ends. Kant is less clear in describing what this necessary role of ends must be. In this regard, he speaks of subjective and objective ends. He speaks of ends as the determining grounds of the will, though he also says they may be but need not be the determining grounds of the will, and he calls ends the subjective determining grounds of the will. I consider each claim in its turn.

First, Kant makes several strong claims about the necessity of ends in ethics. He states that pure practical reason:

> is a faculty of ends [*ein Vermögen der Zwecke*] in general. For practical reason to be indifferent to ends, i.e., to take no interest in them, would be a contradiction; for then it would not determine the maxims of actions (and the actions always contain an end [*Zweck*]) and, consequently, would not be practical reason (MM,54-55/6,395).

The claim is that practical reason by nature involves ends and were it to ignore ends, it would no longer be practical reason. It is necessary for practical reason to take an interest in ends. Similar assertions are made in Kant's other works on ethics. In the *Critique of Practical Reason*, he says, "the will [*den Willen*] could be defined as the faculty of ends [*das Vermögen der Zwecke*]" (CPR,61/5,58-59). He states: "it is certainly undeniable that every volition [*alles Wollen*] must have an object [*Gegenstand*] and therefore a material [*Materie*]" (CPR,34/5,34). In the *Groundwork*, Kant claims: "Rational nature [*Die vernünftige Natur*] separates itself out from all other things by the fact that it sets itself an end [*einen Zweck setzt*]" (Gr.105/4,437). Finally, in the *Metaphysics of Morals*, Kant contrasts the doctrine of right, which proceeds from the end to the maxim, with ethics, which begins with the maxim in order to find the end. He concludes: "Thus in ethics the concept of duty will lead to ends [*auf Zwecke leiten*]" (MM,40/6,382). Ethics cannot begin with ends but it does inevitably lead to ends.

These claims are echoed by similar ones in *Theory and Practice* and in *Religion*. In *Theory and Practice*, Kant says, "without an end there cannot be any *will* [*ohne allen Zweck kann kein Wille sein*]" (TP,46-47n/8,279). In *Religion*, he states that, "in the absence of all reference to an end no determination of the will [*keine Willensbestimmung*] can take place in man" (Rel.4/6,4).

What all of these passages have in common is the claim that the faculty which makes possible ethics is defined by its concern with ends. Practical reason, the will, and rational nature posit ends. Every act of willing, every determination of the will, requires ends. Practical reason has to do with or leads up to ends. Combining this with Kant's earlier definition of end, he is saying that practical reason, and, in fact, every act of willing, necessarily has a material, an object. Ends are a natural correlate of the will.

There is one other way in which Kant emphasizes the centrality of ends to ethics. He focuses on the necessary relationship between actions and ends in contrast to the above point where he looks at the relationship between practical reason, the will, and ends. Hence, Kant argues, the nature of an act involves ends. The long quote above from the *Metaphysics of Morals* says, "actions always contain an end." An action necessarily has a material, an object. In an earlier passage in the *Metaphysics of Morals*, he says, "Accordingly, every action has its end [*jede handlung hat also ihren Zweck*]" (MM,42/6,385).

In short, ends are important to ethics. Kant believes that all willing has an end and that all actions have ends and thus, ethics involves ends. There is a necessary connection therefore between ethics and ends such that it would be false to say that Kant's ethic (or any ethic for that matter) takes no interest in or does not involve ends. The question now is, what is this necessary role of ends in Kant's ethic. On this issue, Kant's answer is less clear. Let me begin with Kant's claims about ends and objects of inclination. Before turning to what role ends serve in ethics, more must be said about what an end is, since what an end is likely has some effect on what an end does.

First, are ends always objects of inclination? Is it the case that the notion of end is tied to that of inclination? These are important questions for the following reason. From the above, it follows that an end is the object or matter of the will. If ends are always objects of inclination, then the object of the will is always an object of inclination. If however, ends are not always objects of inclination, then the object of the will need not be tied to inclination. The question is what sort of thing may serve as the matter of the will. If the matter of the will, the end, is always an object of inclination we would expect Kant's rejection of it as a moral consideration to be complete. But if the matter of the will, the end, need not be an object of inclination, it is possible Kant might find it to be an important moral consideration.

It was shown in section I that Kant in some places identifies an end with an object of inclination. He says: "An *end* [*Zweck*] is always the object of an *inclination* [*der Gegenstand einer Zuneigung*], that is, of an immediate craving for possession of a thing through one's action" (Rel.6n/6,6). He claims: "Now an action done from duty has to set aside altogether the influence of inclination [*den Einfluss der Neigung*] and along with inclination every object of the will [*jeden Gegenstand des Willens*]" (Gr.68/4,400). It looks as if ends or objects of the will are by definition objects of inclination.

If this is Kant's final word on the subject then it is quite understandable why some have seen Kant's claims about principles and duty to entail a rejection of ends. If ends are all sensible ends, then to act out of duty to a principle is precisely not to take into account ends. But this is not all Kant says about ends. What he goes on to say makes two further points about ends. First, not all ends are sensible ends. In spite of the two passages above, Kant describes ends which are not objects of inclination. Thus, if the tie between end and inclination is broken, then those ends which are not objects of inclination may have some value even in an ethic governed by principle. In sum, the opposition between an ethic of principles and an ethic of ends may break down. Second, even if ends were always objects of inclination and so the opposition between principles and ends were to stand up, it would still be possible for Kant to speak positively of ends albeit outside of the realm of ethics. This Kant continues on to do. That is, even ends of inclination may be good or of value simply because human beings naturally have such ends, although in this case, they ought not to be confused with what is of moral value.

Kant makes several additional claims about the nature and the role of ends. But first consider one further point about Kant's language in the above passage. There he says that the end is always an object of inclination which is "an immediate craving for possession of a thing through one's action" (Rel.6n/6,6). This passage seems to identify ends as objects a person desires to possess via his or her action. Ends thus are objects whose possession a person is trying to attain through his or her action. This language of "possession" and "attainment through one's action" suggests a meaning of end that Kant goes on to qualify just as he does the linking of end with inclination. Contrary to what is suggested in this passage, Kant argues that ends are not always objects attained or possessed in the sense of produced through a person's action. Ends need not be the sort of objects that must be effected by or produced by an action. They may be objects with existence in themselves, that is, self-existing (Gr.95-96/4,428). There is more on this distinction in what follows.

Next, there is evidence which suggests that Kant does not mean for ends to be synonymous with objects of inclination. This evidence comes from the *Groundwork* and the *Metaphysics of Morals*. Put briefly, the point is this. Kant lays out a distinction between subjective and objective ends or between technical and moral ends such that he recognizes that there are ends which are not objects of inclination. This recognition enables ends to be seen as something other than sensible objects desired by human inclinations.

In the *Groundwork*, Kant speaks of a difference between "subjective ends [*subjectiven Zwecken*], which are based on impulsions, and objective [*objectiven*] ends, which depend on motives valid for every rational being" (Gr.95/4,427). He goes on to distinguish them in this way:

> All the objects of inclination have only a conditioned value; for if there were not these inclinations and the needs grounded on them, their object would be valueless . . . Thus the value of all objects that can *be produced* by our action is always conditioned . . . Rational beings, on the other hand, are called *persons* because their nature already marks them out as ends in themselves . . . Persons, therefore, are not merely subjective ends [*nicht bloss subjective Zwecke*] whose existence as an object of our actions has a value *for us*: they are *objective ends*—that is, things whose existence is in itself an end [*objective Zwecke, d.i. Dinge, deren Dasein an sich selbst Zweck ist*] (Gr.95-96/4,428).

Thus, subjective ends are objects of inclination which have only a relative value. The inclinations that aim to realize or produce these subjective ends are peculiar to human beings, not rational beings. So, these subjective ends become valuable to human beings as goals of their inclinations but they have no absolute moral value. Objective ends, on the other hand, are ends in themselves and have absolute value because of what they are and not because human beings desire them.

A little further on, Kant specifies that in the idea of person or humanity

> humanity [*die Menschheit*] is conceived, not as an end of man (subjectively) [*als Zweck der Menschen (subjectiv)*]—that is, as an object which, as a matter of fact, happens to be made an end—but as an objective end [*als objectiver Zweck*]—one which, be our ends what they may, must, as a law, constitute the supreme limiting condition of all subjective ends and so must spring from pure reason [*aus reiner Vernunft entspringen muss*] (Gr.98/4,431).

This passage makes it clear that objective ends arise from pure reason and not inclination. In addition to those subjective ends proposed by the sensible impulses, there are objective ends dictated by pure reason. Kant calls the objective end "humanity" or "rational beings" or "persons." What is crucial here is that Kant has said that the source of an end need not be inclination and that there is such an end whose source is not inclination.

The same point is made in the *Metaphysics of Morals*. Kant states that ethics supplies:

> a matter (an object of free choice), namely, an *end* of pure reason [*einen Zweck der reinen Vernunft*] which is at the same time represented as an objectively necessary end, i.e., as a duty for man. For since sensible inclinations [*die sinnlichen Neigungen*] may misdirect us to ends (the matter of choice) which may be contrary to duty, legislative reason cannot guard against their influence other than, in turn, by means of an opposing moral end [*moralischen Zweck*], which therefore must be given a priori independently of inclination (MM,37-38/6,380-81).

Similarly, he claims:

> we are here concerned not with the ends which man makes for himself according to the sensible impulses [*sinnlichen Antrieben*] of his nature, but, rather, with objects of his free choice under its own laws-objects which he ought to make his end. One may call the former the technical (subjective), properly speaking pragmatic doctrine of ends . . . but the latter must be called the moral (objective) doctrine of ends [*die moralische (objective) Zwecklehre*] (MM,43/6,385).

Again, Kant is offering a distinction between types of ends. Quite apart from the ends provided by sensible inclinations or impulses, there are moral ends, ends of pure reason, objective ends. Kant goes on to identify the moral ends as one's own perfection and the happiness of others (ibid.).[3] He also argues that there must be such a moral end because without one, all ends would be only subjective, that is, they would be ends people happen to choose for themselves. If all ends are only subjective then a categorical imperative is impossible and so the doctrine of morals would be destroyed (ibid.).

There is also some indirect evidence in *Theory and Practice* that not all ends are objects of inclination. There too Kant seems to take it for granted that some ends are moral and some are not. He says, "Not every end [*Zweck*] is moral, however" (TP,47n/8,279). If not *every* end is moral, there is nonetheless *an* end or perhaps *some* ends that are moral. It follows that there are different types of ends and since not all ends are of the same type (not all are moral) it seems that not all ends are objects of inclination.

Hence, the central point is clear; not all ends are objects of inclination. Some ends owe their source to something other than inclination (pure reason) and so have a necessity about them that is lacking to other types of ends. There are therefore moral objective ends posited by pure reason. However, it is obvious that Kant makes inconsistent claims about ends. He says all ends are objects of inclination and he says not all ends are objects of inclination. The issue now is whether there is any reason to prefer one of these accounts over the other.

There are such reasons and the latter claim, that not all ends are objects of inclination, is more consistent with the whole of Kant's complex ethic. The reasons are two. First, the passages in which Kant argues that ends are always objects of inclination occur in *Religion* (in a footnote) and early on in the *Groundwork*. Evidence for the opposite claim comes from later on in the *Groundwork* and in the *Metaphysics of Morals*. The *Religion* is not one of Kant's major works on ethics and so it would not be surprising if the clearest formulation of his view of ends appeared in another work. Also, the context for the passage from early on in the *Groundwork* is a discussion of moral worth and inclination, not ends. There Kant says that an action done from duty must put aside inclination and along with it every object of the will. Perhaps the point is not to link objects or ends with inclination but rather to see that both objects and inclination are excluded from serving as the ground for moral willing.

Second, the claim that ends need not be objects of inclination accords better with Kant's overall system of ethics than the claim that they must be objects of inclination. If ends were indeed only objects of inclination, why would Kant spend much time talking about them? Instead, he spends a great deal of time talking about ends; for instance, the ends of humanity, one's own perfection, the happiness of others, the good will, the highest good. Similarly, if ends were indeed only objects of inclination, why would Kant have formulated one version of the supreme principle of morality in terms of an end (which he has done)? In other words, if ends are objects of inclination, then the moral law ought not be stated in terms of ends since that would reduce it to the level of inclination. Instead, in his second formulation of the moral law, Kant speaks of ends, that is, of rational beings as ends (Gr.104/4,436). All of Kant's talk about ends and his statement of the moral law in terms of ends is proof that ends need not be objects of inclination.

Now that it is clear what Kant means by ends, the next issue is the role of ends in his ethic. Specifically, do ends always act as determining grounds of the will? That is, is it the job of ends to determine the will to action or do ends sometimes function in such a way that they do not determine the will to action?

This is an important question for the following reason. It was shown above that ends are the content, the matter, the object, of the will. Furthermore, the matter or object of the will can be given either by inclination or by pure reason. Whatever is the source of an end, it remains the case that the end is the matter of the will. The question now is how this matter of the will is to serve with regard to the determination of the will. The obvious answer, given Kant's emphasis on the form of the law, is that ends need not determine the will. The maxim of a will may have content without that content having to be the reason for the will's action. In spite of this apparently obvious answer, there are passages in which Kant states that ends are (always act as) determining grounds of the will. If an end is always that which determines a will to act, then it seems to follow that all acts are materially motivated, in other words, heteronomous. Kant says, "Wherever an object of the will [*ein Object des Willens*] has to be put down as the basis for prescribing a rule to determine the will, there the rule is heteronomy" (Gr.111/4,444). But surely, Kant is not suggesting that all rules are heteronomous. Kant's claims about whether ends serve to determine the will must be looked at in order to clarify the role played by ends.

In several places, Kant states that ends determine the will, in other words, act as determining grounds of the will. In the *Metaphysics of Morals*, he says:

> An end is an object of choice (of a rational being); by means of the representation of such an end, choice is determined to an action to produce the object (MM,38/6,381).[4]

> the representation of the end determines choice to an action whereby the object is produced (MM,42/6,384).

Thus, it appears that an end has the task of determining a will to a certain action.

The same point is made in the second *Critique* although there Kant seems to recognize the danger in this view. To wit, the claim that ends, as the matter of the will, determine the will leads to heteronomy. He states:

> the will could be defined as the faculty of ends, since they are always determining grounds of the faculty of desire according to principles (CPR,61/5,58-59).[5]

> An end, however, as an object which precedes and contains the ground of determination of the will by a practical rule—that is, an end as the material of the will—is, if taken as a determining ground of the will, only empirical; it could thus serve for the Epicurean principle in the happiness theory but never as a pure rational principle of ethics and duty (CPR,42/5,41).[6]

These passages too suggest that ends are objects which determine the will. In the second passage Kant is somewhat more guarded. He seems to try to resist concluding that an end must be the determining ground of the will since he sees that to make an end the ground of the will's principle takes away from the rationality, the pureness of the principle. However, there are two problems here. First, there is the fact that this passage identifies an end which contains the determining ground of the will with an end as the material of the will. The tone of the passage implies that perhaps ends need not act as determining grounds of the will and so heteronomy could be avoided. But it was shown above that an end is always the material of the will and if that is equivalent to being a determining ground of the will, then all ends are determining grounds of the will. Second, it is not strictly true to say that an end as material determining ground of the will is only "empirical" if by empirical Kant means sensible, not rational. Ends are material in the sense that they are the object, the content, of the will. But they need not be empirical, that is, nonrational, in that they can be posited by pure reason (they can be objective ends). In short, these two passages also point to the identification of ends with determining grounds of the will.

Finally, in the *Groundwork*, Kant gives the impression that ends are the determining grounds of the will's principles. He says: "Now what serves the will as a subjective ground of its self-determination is an *end*" (Gr.95/4,427).[7] Kant here calls an end that which serves as a ground for the determination of the will.[8] He goes on to speak of the relation of ends to hypothetical and categorical imperatives. He says that relative ends, ends adopted arbitrarily by a rational being, can ground only hypothetical imperatives (Gr.95/4,428). However, if there is to be a categorical imperative "it must be such that from the idea of something which is necessarily an end [*Zweck*] for every one because it is an *end in itself* it forms an *objective* principle of the will [*ein objectives Princip des Willens ausmacht*] and consequently can serve as a practical law" (Gr.96/4,428-29). The point seems to be that both hypothetical and categorical imperatives are based on, grounded on, ends, though different sorts of ends. Kant speaks about

> something which as *an end in itself* could be a ground of determinate laws . . . and in it alone, would there be the ground of a possible categorical imperative (Gr.95/4,428).[9]

Kant is speaking as if ends act as the determining ground of the will in formulating both hypothetical and categorical imperatives.[10]

However, there are in Kant's texts claims to the contrary. There are statements that maintain that ends need not and even should not act as determining grounds of the will. The difficulty is as follows. The passages from above define an end as that which acts as a determining ground of the will. The passages to follow claim that an end need not act as a determining ground of the will. If this is the case, then an end cannot be defined as that which determines the will. What is not at issue is whether ends sometimes serve as determining grounds of the will. What is at issue is whether ends must always serve as determining grounds of the will.

In the *Metaphysics of Morals*, Kant suggests that ends do not always ground or determine the will's principles. His reason is that sometimes the ends result from the principles. This seems to mean that sometimes it is the will's principle that does the grounding in that it grounds or determines the ends. He says:

> Thus in ethics the concept of duty will lead to ends [*auf Zwecke leiten*], and the maxims regarding the ends which we ought to set before ourselves must be founded on moral principles [*nach moralischen Grundsätzen begründen müssen*] (MM,40/6,382).
>
> the moral doctrine of ends, which treat of duties, rests on a priori principles given in pure practical reason (MM,43/6,385).[11]

Kant is claiming that ends do not always determine principles because it is principles which lead to ends.

The point is made even more forcefully in the second *Critique*. Here Kant says quite explicitly that the object of the will, the end, need not act as the determining ground of the will.

> The material of a practical principle is the object of the will. This object either is the determining ground of the will or it is not (CPR,26/5,27).[12]
>
> every volition must have an object and therefore a material; but the material cannot be supposed, for this reason, to be the determining ground and condition of the maxim (CPR,34/5,34).

> The moral law is the sole determining ground of the pure will [*der alleinige Bestimmungsgrund des reinen Willens*]. Since it is merely formal, requiring only that the form of the maxim be universally legislative, as a determining ground it abstracts from all material and thus from every object of volition (CPR,113/5,109).

These three passages though they do not use the term end make a point about the role of ends. That which is the object or material or end of the will may or may not ground the will's principle. The fact that the will has an object is not an indication that the object has conditioned the will. It is open to ends to act as determining grounds of the will. If they so act, however, the result is heteronomy. Hence, it is also open to ends not to serve as determining grounds of the will. In fact, Kant says, for a moral principle or a pure will, the determining ground must not be an object or a material.

This is the Kant with which readers are most familiar. This is "Kant the formalist" who insists that whatever else ends may contribute to ethics, their job is not to ground the pure will.[13] In the *Groundwork*, Kant makes similarly decisive claims about the role of ends. Let us consider these claims before trying to resolve Kant's apparently inconsistent statements concerning the task of ends.

As the following examples show, Kant often speaks as if ends ought not to have any connection with categorical imperatives. Thus, not only is the categorical imperative not grounded on an end but it ought to abstract entirely from ends. So, he claims that moral worth can be found only "*in the principle of the will*, irrespective of the ends [*der Zwecke*] which can be brought about by such an action" (Gr.68/4,400). A categorical imperative "declares an action to be objectively necessary in itself without reference to some purpose—that is, even without any further end [*einen andern Zweck*]" (Gr.82/4,415). Finally, Kant says, a categorical imperative "is concerned, not with the matter of the action and its presumed results, but with its form and with the principle from which it follows" (Gr.84/4,416).

These passages from the *Groundwork* reiterate the claims made in the *Metaphysics of Morals* and in the second *Critique*. It is not the case that ends always serve as determining grounds of the will. It is especially the case that categorical imperatives and duties do not have their ground in ends, that is, in objects. Ends may result from or be present in moral principles but they do not determine moral principles.

The question now is what to do about these seemingly inconsistent claims about ends. Are ends always determining grounds of the will or are they not? To answer the question we must rethink the way it is posed. That is, the question has assumed that the answer must be either "yes, ends always act as determining grounds of the will" (though then there is the problem of heteronomy) or "no, ends do not always act as determining grounds of the will" (though then there is the problem of Kant's claims to the contrary). No doubt Kant has contributed to the view that this is an either/or situation. In some places, Kant seems to believe that either ends determine the will or they do not, in which case only the form of the maxim determines the will. There is a material determining ground of the will or there is a formal determining ground of the will. For instance, he says:

> a free will must find its ground of determination in the law, but independently of the material [*Materie*] of the law. But besides the latter there is nothing in a law except the legislative form [*Form*]. Therefore, the legislative form, in so far as it is contained in the maxim, is the only thing which can constitute a determining ground of the (free) will (CPR,28-29/5,29).

The implication is that a choice must be made between material grounds of the will, ends, and formal grounds of the will. Any of the will's principles grounded on ends will be heteronomous while those principles grounded on the form of the maxim will be autonomous. But in fact, this is not an either/or choice. As was shown above, ends are not all of the same kind. Some are chosen by the senses, but some are posited by pure reason. It cannot be said that ends are by nature empirical or sensible. Given the presence of ends of pure reason, it is possible that ends might work in conjunction with the form of the maxim to determine the will. This, in fact, is what happens. To put it simply, ends always act as determining grounds of the will but for categorical imperatives, they are not *the* or the *only* or the *direct* determining ground of the will. For an autonomous will, ends always work in conjunction with the form of the maxim to determine the will. In an autonomous will, the ends of pure reason act to determine the will because they follow from the will. Hence, they are not the direct determining ground of the will or the first determining ground of the will or the sole determining ground of the will. These ends of pure reason can determine the will indirectly, in conjunction with, and because they follow from, the moral law.[14]

There are places in which Kant hints at this conclusion and then there are two places in which he makes this conclusion explicit. First, there are several passages in the second *Critique* that suggest that it may not be an either/or situation (either a formal determining ground of the will or a material determining ground of the will). These passages can be interpreted as allowing that the moral will may not have only formal determining grounds. Consider the way Kant characterizes the determining ground of the will in these passages:

1. The mere form of a universal legislation, which is possible through our maxims, must constitute the supreme and *direct* [*unmittelbaren*] determining ground of the will (CPR,42/5,41; emphasis mine).
2. This *Critique* concerns itself only with whether and how reason . . . can *directly* [*unmittelbar*] determine the will (CPR,47/5,46; emphasis mine).

3. The moral law has been established by itself and justified as the *direct* [*unmittelbarer*] determining ground of the will (CPR,67/5,64; emphasis mine).
4. For how a law in itself can be the *direct* [*unmittelbar*] determining ground of the will (which is the essence of morality) is an insoluble problem for the human reason (CPR,75/5,72; emphasis mine).

Kant is claiming here that the form of the moral law, and pure practical reason, and the moral law itself are the direct determining grounds of the will. The hint lies in what is not said. If there is a direct determining ground of the will, perhaps there is an indirect determining ground of the will. Or, in any case, if there is only to be one determining ground of the will, why bother to qualify it as a direct determining ground? What is Kant aiming to distinguish this formal determining ground *from* by calling it a direct ground? Kant does not explain although the possibility certainly exists that in specifying that the form, the law, is the direct determining ground of the will, Kant is making room for the fact that some material, some ends (the ends of pure reason) are indirect determining grounds of the will. By suggesting a distinction between direct and indirect determining grounds of the will, Kant allows a place for ends as determining grounds of the will without compromising the priority of the law as determining ground of the will. At least there is this hint that it may be possible to have both formal determining grounds of the will and material determining grounds of the will.

There is another hint in the second *Critique* that formal determining grounds may not exclude material determining grounds. Perhaps Kant is not saying that in a moral action ends can never act as determining grounds of the will. Perhaps instead he is only insisting that in a moral action ends can never act as the first determining grounds of the will. That is, if an action is to be moral, ends cannot supplant, precede, or come before the moral law as that which determines the will. So ends may not be wholly excluded as determining grounds but they can be only secondary determining grounds.[15] This conclusion is at least possible in the following passages.

1. when we assume any object . . . as the determining ground of the will *prior* to [*vor*] the moral law . . . this always produces heteronomy (CPR,113/5,109; emphasis mine).
2. An end, however, as an object which *precedes* [*vor*] and contains the ground of determination of the will . . . is, if taken as a determining ground of the will, only empirical (CPR,42/5,41; emphasis mine).

In other words, if ends *precede* the moral law as determining grounds of the will, the result is heteronomy, not morality. But perhaps, if ends *follow* from the moral law as determining grounds of the will, the result is still morality. Ends, as material determining grounds of the will, need not be absent from moral actions though they cannot be prior to formal determining grounds of the will. Thus, here is another hint that in a moral action there may be both formal determining grounds and material determining grounds.

Second, in the *Metaphysics of Morals*, Kant distinguishes between the doctrine of right which has to do with "consistency with itself when its maxim is made into a universal law" and ethics which provides "in addition a matter (an object of free choice), namely, an *end* of pure reason [*einen Zweck der reinen Vernunft*] which is at the same time represented as an objectively necessary end" (MM,37/6,380). This distinction in essence separates the formal ground of determination from the material ground of determination. But Kant continues:

> If, however, I am also obligated to make something which lies in the concepts of practical reason an end for myself, and if, therefore, besides the formal determining ground [*formalen Bestimmungsgrunde*] of choice (such as right contains) I am obligated to have in addition a material

> determining ground [*noch einen materialen*], i.e., an end that can be opposed to the end derived from sensible impulses, then this would be the concept of an end which is in itself a duty (MM,38/6,381).

Kant is saying that if there are ends of pure reason (which he goes on to identify) then besides, that is, in addition to, a formal determining ground of the will, there is a material determining ground of the will. So if ends can be ends of pure reason, there is no reason to have to choose between a material determining ground of the will and a formal determining ground of the will. The will can have both. It is possible to distinguish then: heteronomous principles, principles of right, and ethical principles. The first have only a material determining ground of the will, the second have only a formal determining ground of the will, and the third have both formal and material determining grounds. Kant avoids the charge of heteronomy in ethical principles even though these ethical principles have a material ground in the following way. First, the end that is the material ground for ethical principles is not an empirical, sensible end. It is an end of pure reason. Second, the material ground of an ethical principle is not the sole ground of the principle. The material ground does not by itself or directly determine the will. It is a corollary to the formal ground, that is, another way of describing wherein lies the necessity of the principle.

The second place Kant makes this point explicit is in the *Groundwork*. He states:

> That is to say, the ground for every enactment of practical law lies *objectively in the rule* and in the form of universality which (according to our first principle) makes the rule capable of being a law (and indeed a law of nature); *subjectively*, however, it lies in the *end* [*im Zwecke*]; but (according to our second principle) the subject of all ends is to be found in every rational being as an end in himself (Gr.98/4,431).

> The principle 'So act in relation to every rational being (both to yourself and to others) that he may at the same time count in your maxim as an end in himself' is thus at bottom the same as the principle 'Act on a maxim which at the same time contains in itself its own universal validity for every rational being' (Gr.105/4,437-38).

> It is, however, better if in moral *judgement* we proceed always in accordance with the strict method and take as our basis the universal formula of the categorical imperative: '*Act on the maxim which can at the same time be made a universal law*' (Gr.104/4,436-37).

Kant's claim here is basically the same as it was in the *Metaphysics of Morals*. A practical law, the categorical imperative, has both an objective and a subjective ground (called in the *Metaphysics of Morals*, a formal and a material ground). The categorical imperative can be formulated objectively in terms of its form or subjectively in terms of its end.[16] Kant feels that at times it is "better" (safer? less confusing?) to focus on the objective formulation of the categorical imperative though he acknowledges that in essence the objective formulation of the imperative is the same as the subjective formulation.

The conclusion these passages point to is that ends *do* act as determining grounds of the will. Whenever there are ends present, they act in a way to ground the will's principles. Sometimes ends are arbitrarily chosen, sensible objects and serve as the sole ground of hypothetical principles. On the other hand, sometimes ends are posited as necessary by pure reason and serve as a ground of categorical imperatives in conjunction with other formal grounds. This conclusion about ends has these two consequences. First, it shows that Kant's various claims about the role of ends can be consistent. Yes, ends are always determining grounds of the will, but also, no, ends are not always *the* determining ground of the will in the sense of the sole or exclusive determining ground. Sometimes ends are the sole determining ground of the will and hence hypothetical imperatives result. On the other hand, sometimes ends are not the only determining ground of the will and so categorical imperatives result. Kant would surely insist that no end however valuable in itself is ever the sole ground of a categorical imperative since that same imperative must also be subject to an objective, formal determining ground.[17]

Second, this conclusion suggests that ends have a recognized place of importance in Kant's ethics. At least part of what the moral law does is to posit an objectively necessary end of pure reason. The recognition of this end as the material of the will is crucial to finite rational beings. This end is the subjective ground for their (our) enactment of the moral law. In the *Metaphysics of Morals*, Kant identifies this end as one that can be opposed to the end derived from sensible impulses. Part of the role for this end of pure reason may be to counter the lure of the sensible end and for finite rational beings to allow for a material determining ground, albeit of a certain type and acting at a certain time. The ends of pure reason are important perhaps not in a purely formal ethic but certainly in an ethic for finite rational beings. Finite rational beings act for the sake of these ends (and not simply for the sake of universality) and use them to oppose and hold off the attractions of sensible ends. In acting for the sake of these ends, they (we) do so because the ends are dictated by and follow from (and hence, are secondary to) the moral law. However, the ends of pure reason point to the finite side of Kant's ethic by emphasizing the place of a material determining ground for which the agent may act and against which sensible ends work.

This section has aimed at clarifying the role of ends in Kant's ethic. It considered the way Kant defines practical reason and action in terms of ends, the distinction between objective and subjective ends, and the ways in which ends can act as determining grounds of the will. Now let me relate this talk of ends to the issue of happiness.

III. Happiness As Natural End

On the question of happiness as a natural desire of human beings, Kant's views are quite simple in spite of the fact that some have not understood them. Kant clearly identifies happiness as a natural and inevitable end of human beings. He sees that in this role as natural end, happiness is of value. It is not to be renounced. It is not evil. Lastly, he insists that while happiness is of value, its pursuit is not a moral duty. That is, happiness is not an objective end and so in no way can human beings construe that one of their duties is the pursuit of their natural end of happiness.

In all of Kant's major works on ethics, there are reminders of the inevitability of a human being's desire for happiness. In the *Lectures on Ethics*, there is reference to "the universal end of man, that is, happiness" (LE,4/M,5). In the *Groundwork*, he says: "all men have already of themselves the strongest and deepest inclination towards happiness" (Gr.67/4,399), "every man wants to attain happiness" (Gr.85/4,418), "the natural end which all men seek is their own happiness" (Gr.98/4,430). Hence, Kant concludes:

> There is, however, *one* end that can be presupposed as actual in all rational beings (so far as they are dependent beings to whom imperatives apply); and thus there is one purpose which they not only *can* have, but which we can assume with certainty that they all *do* have by a natural necessity—the purpose, namely, of *happiness* (Gr.83/4,415).

Kant recognizes that the desire for happiness is a trait peculiar to finite rational nature. It is because human beings are rational and sensible that they naturally wish for happiness. In the second *Critique*, Kant says: "To be happy is necessarily the desire of every rational but finite being" (CPR,24/5,25). In *Religion*, he claims: "By our *nature* as beings dependent upon circumstances of sensibility, we crave happiness first and unconditionally" (Rel.41n/6,46). Later while discussing the hope for and the promise of the kingdom of God, Kant states that happiness "constitutes the other part of what man inevitably wishes" (Rel.125/6,134).

What can be found again and again in Kant's texts are claims about the inevitability and the naturalness of a person's desire for happiness. There is no doubt that Kant considers the desire for happiness to be a fact about the sensible side of our finite rational nature. Happiness is and forever will be posited as an end by human beings. Perhaps two passages in the *Metaphysics of Morals* put the point most simply:

> one's own happiness is an end which, to be sure, all men do have (by virtue of the impulse of their nature) (MM,43/6,386).
>
> It is inevitable for human nature that one should wish for and seek happiness (MM,45/6,387).

However, these assertions about happiness as a natural end for human beings say nothing about the value of happiness as a natural end. It is possible that Kant, having once identified happiness as a natural end, might have gone on to decry it. He might have then said that happiness as a natural end was to be despised or worked against or condemned or labelled as evil. But he did none of these things. Instead, he offers three evaluations of happiness: it ought not be renounced, it is not evil, and it is good.

First, Kant maintains in at least two places that the correct response to happiness is not to condemn it. Just because happiness is an end posited by a person's sensible nature does not mean that a person ought to work to give it up. Kant believes that his emphasis on duty and the moral law does not entail the condemning of a natural end like happiness but only the restraining of the desire for that end. Thus, the object of happiness is not necessarily disvalued in the process of focusing on the form of the moral law. Happiness is not necessarily worthless or deserving of condemnation, it is simply set aside. Hence, the first thing Kant says pertaining to the value of happiness is that happiness need not be renounced. He states:

> pure practical reason does not require that we should renounce [*aufgeben*] the claims to happiness (CPR,96/5,93).

> My definition [of ethics as a science that teaches how we are to become worthy of happiness], as I had not failed to note, does not mean that in matters of obeying duty a man should *renounce* [*entsagen*] his natural goal of happiness. He cannot do so, nor can any other finite rational being. What I mean is that, when duty calls, he must completely *abstract* from this consideration (TP,45-46/8,278).

Second, Kant goes a bit further and insists that a human being's natural end is not evil. Kant denies that a person's sensuous side, his or her inclinations, are the cause of evil. He says that the ground of evil "cannot be placed . . . in man's sensuous nature and the natural inclinations arising therefrom" (Rel.30/6,34). For, "these are not directly related to evil" (ibid.). Thus, happiness, a person's inevitable and natural end, is not evil. Kant concludes that evil "is to be sought not in his inclinations, but in his perverted maxim, and so in freedom itself. Those inclinations merely make difficult the *execution* of the good maxim which opposes them" (Rel.51n/6,58).

Finally, Kant believes happiness is not only not evil but in fact good. For instance, in the first *Critique*, he speaks about not losing sight "of the supreme end, the happiness of all mankind" (A851/B879). Granted Kant is talking here about more than a person's own happiness which is what he has identified as the natural end of all human beings. Yet, a person's own happiness is no doubt included in the happiness of all mankind and so is at least a part of the supreme end. Surely, something that was of no value or of negative value would not play a part in that which is of supreme value. Hence, it seems evident that a person's own happiness is of positive value as an end. Kant acknowledges this most clearly in the following passage:

> Natural inclinations, *considered in themselves*, are *good*, that is, not a matter of reproach, and it is not only futile to want to extirpate them but to do so would also be harmful and blameworthy. Rather, let them be tamed and instead of clashing with one another they can be brought into harmony in a wholeness which is called happiness (Rel.51/6,58).

The claim that Kant values happiness as a natural end is certainly not an original one. Many of Kant's commentators have seen that happiness as naturally desired by human beings is good.[18] However, others have failed to see this point. In general, what distinguishes this account of the value of happiness from other accounts is that it places the positive value of happiness as a natural end in a broader context. It argues that this view is neither the whole of Kant's account of happiness nor is it the most positive thing he says about happiness. The claim that happiness is of value as a natural end is a step towards the more encompassing claim that happiness is necessarily bound up in many ways with Kant's system of ethics (A809/B837).

There is however a warning that appears repeatedly in Kant's comments on happiness as a natural end. Though happiness is a natural end for human beings, its pursuit is *not* thereby a duty. The *Lectures on Ethics* states: "The duties we owe to ourselves do not depend on the relation of the action to the ends of happiness" (LE,120-21/M,150). In the third *Critique*, Kant speaks of happiness as pleasantness [*Annehmlichkeit*] and pleasantness as enjoyment [*Genuss*] (CJ,42/5,208). Kant concludes that: "An obligation to enjoyment is a manifest absurdity" (CJ,43n/5,209).

Perhaps it is Kant's insistence that there is no duty to pursue happiness as a natural end that has convinced some that Kant does not value happiness. But these are two separate issues. The question of what a person's duties are is not the sole or exclusive concern of ethics. There are subjective ends and objective ends, ends of inclination and ends of reason, objects human beings happen to desire and objects human beings ought to desire. Kant has allowed that the subjective end of happiness is good (as are objective ends) but not that it is thereby the object of a moral duty (as are objective ends). In *Theory and Practice*, Kant specifies that the end of happiness is not a moral end. He states: "Not every end is moral, however (not, for example, that of one's own happiness)" (TP,46-47n/8,279-80). Hence, while the end of happiness is good, it is not a moral end and so its pursuit is not the object of a moral duty. In the *Metaphysics of Morals*, Kant speaks of those who set up "a supposed obligation to take care of my own (physical) happiness and so make this, which is my natural and merely subjective end, into a duty (an objective end)" (MM,46/6,388). This view, he says, "needs to be set right" (ibid.). Setting this view right involves recognizing that "this end [one's own happiness] can never without contradiction be regarded as a duty" (MM,43/6,386). In short, "happiness is not an end which is at the same time a duty" (MM,45/6,387). These are the conclusions Kant reaches concerning happiness as an end. Chapter 4 reveals that he arrives at quite a different conclusion regarding happiness as a means.

Chapter Four

The Positive Role of Happiness As Means

Let us consider Kant's treatment of happiness as a means [*Mittel*], not an end [*Zweck*]. In its role as means, happiness is not taken to be the object of the will, but rather, something which, although not directly aimed at, aids the will in achieving its object. Happiness thus has a role to play because it enables the will to realize some other end and not because it is or ought to be an end itself.

When discussing happiness in its role as means to some other end, Kant speaks of an "indirect duty." So, the issue of happiness as a means is connected with the question of indirect duties. Kant's talk of an indirect duty to pursue happiness clearly goes beyond the issues of the last chapter. There happiness was recognized to be a natural end of human beings and as such happiness is good although its pursuit is never the object of a duty. Here the perspective changes in two ways. First, happiness is not treated as an end but as a means to some other end. Second, happiness considered as a means is found to be a good and its pursuit the object of a duty, albeit an indirect duty. Happiness considered as a natural end is valuable but not to the extent that happiness as a means is valuable. Happiness in this role comes to play an important part in Kant's ethics as that which helps human beings achieve morality.

Kant speaks of indirect duties in four of his works on ethics: *Lectures on Ethics*, *Groundwork*, *Critique of*

Practical Reason, and *Metaphysics of Morals*. There is explicit mention of an indirect duty to pursue happiness in the *Groundwork*, the second *Critique*, and the *Metaphysics of Morals*. In the *Lectures* and the *Metaphysics of Morals*, Kant gives other examples of indirect duties that are not obviously related to the issue of happiness. I focus on these texts in order to see how they contribute to our understanding of the role of happiness in Kant's ethics.

One other preliminary point must be made. Very few commentators have paid any attention to Kant's concept of an indirect duty or to the role of happiness as a means to some other end. Some critics speak in passing of a person's duty to pursue his or her own happiness.[1] They mention this duty although they do not seem to realize its significance. Even more unfortunate is the fact that most commentators have nothing to say on this topic.[2] But certainly, if there is a class of indirect duties in Kant's system of ethics, a person needs to consider it in order to discover the full range of his or her duties. And if the pursuit of personal happiness is one of those indirect duties, then a person needs to know that in order to understand the role of happiness in ethics.

More specifically, the main point is this. While the description Kant offers of an indirect duty to pursue personal happiness does nothing to alter the basic dichotomies between duty and inclination, or between moral principles and prudential principles, it does radically complicate them. It means that the natural world is not unrelated to the moral world. Natural ends, like happiness, are taken into the realm of morality, recognized to have a new task (that of means to moral ends) and hence come to have a worth they otherwise lack. Thus, more attention needs to be paid to how natural ends and objects of inclination facilitate morality. Natural ends in this new role as means to morality are validated and assigned moral worth as objects of duty. Natural feelings and natural objects seem in fact for Kant to play a crucial pedagogical role in encouraging the pursuit of moral ends. On the other hand, it does not follow that natural ends and inclinations are therefore completely vindicated and valued. Natural ends as ends play no part in morality but as means they contribute to morality. It is in this new role that happiness must be seen to be not ignored by morality but an aid to morality.

The discussion proceeds in this way. Section I looks at the three passages in which happiness is treated as a means and its pursuit is identified as an indirect duty. Kant's statements themselves are quite unambiguous. I consider first what it is for happiness to be a means and exactly how Kant believes it functions as a means. Section II looks at Kant's claim that the pursuit of one's own happiness is an indirect duty. It is because happiness functions as a means that the pursuit of happiness becomes an indirect duty. I consider what it means to be an indirect duty and how committed Kant is to the idea of indirect duties. Section III looks at other examples of indirect duties, namely, those that do not pertain obviously to happiness. In these cases too, it is apparently because an object functions as a means to some other moral end that an indirect duty to act in a certain way toward that object is generated.

I. Happiness As a Means

There are three passages which link the notions of personal happiness, means, and indirect duty. They are these:

1. To assure one's own happiness is a duty (at least indirectly); for discontent with one's state, in a press of cares and amidst unsatisfied wants, might easily become a great *temptation to the transgression of duty* (Gr.67/4,399).[3]

2. It can even be a duty in certain respects to provide for one's happiness in part because (since it includes skill, health, and riches) it contains means to the fulfilment of one's duty and in part because the lack of it

(e.g., poverty) contains temptations to transgress against duty. But to further one's happiness can never be a direct duty and even less can it be a principle of all duty (CPR,96/5,93).[4]

3. Adversity, pain, and want are great temptations to transgress one's duty. Thus it would seem that affluence, strength, health, and welfare in general, which are opposed to those influences, can also be regarded as ends that are at the same time duties; that is to say, it is a duty to promote one's own happiness and not merely that of others. But in that case the end is not happiness [*Glückseligkeit*], but the morality of the subject; and happiness is merely the means of removing the hindrances to morality, permitted means [*Mittel*], that is, since no one has a right to demand from me the sacrifice of those ends of mine that are not immoral. It is not directly a duty to seek affluence for itself; but indirectly it may very well be a duty,[5] namely, in order to guard against poverty, which is a great temptation to vice. But then it is not my happiness, but the preservation of the integrity of my morality, that is my end and at the same time my duty (MM,46/6,388).

First of all, it is evident from these texts that Kant is talking about happiness. It is happiness [*Glückseligkeit*] that Kant is asserting to be a means to something else. Perhaps a critic might claim that there is really more about skill, health, riches, strength, and welfare in general in these texts than there is about happiness. But, in fact, in all these passages, Kant explicitly links the term happiness to his talk of skill, health, riches, and so forth. In addition, as shown in chapter 1, happiness is precisely this satisfaction of inclinations and wants which include skill, health, riches, and so forth. So it is clear that Kant is positing a new role for happiness, that of means to some other end.

In statements (2) and (3) above, happiness is referred to as a means [*Mittel*]. In the *Groundwork*, Kant defines a "means" this way: "What, on the other hand, contains merely the ground of the possibility of an action whose effect is an end is called a *means* [*das Mittel*]" (Gr.95/4,427). Happiness as a means thus makes possible an action whose effect is an end. This means that happiness is a way of achieving some other end. It of course does not follow that happiness is necessarily the *sole* way of achieving this other end.[6] Happiness in its role as means is a facilitator, an aid, made use of because it makes it possible for the will to act in a way to achieve the will's end.

Now there is no secret about the identity of this end to which happiness is a means. Kant's answer is most clear in passage (3) from above. The end to which happiness is a means is "the morality of the subject" or "the integrity of my morality." Passage (2) calls the end "the fulfilment of one's duty." Similarly, in other passages that refer to means and indirect duties, Kant identifies the end as "man" (LE,239/M,302), "himself" (MM,106/6,443), and "humanity" (LE,239/M,302).

Kant's point is clear. The state of happiness, Kant maintains, enables a person to be moral. The moral end is man or humanity or morality itself (the good will).[7] In the process of pursuing this moral end, it emerges that there are certain states or objects which facilitate the achievement of the moral end. These intermediate states or objects are known as means and happiness is one such state. Now it is worthwhile to consider exactly how happiness is a means to morality.

Kant claims that there are two ways in which happiness functions as a means to morality. He enumerates these in the second *Critique*:

> It can even be a duty in certain respects to provide for one's happiness, in part because . . . it contains means to the fulfilment of one's duty and in part because the lack of it . . . contains temptations to transgress against duty (CPR,96/5,93).

Kant is claiming that one reason happiness is important is that it helps in the achievement of morality. The second reason happiness is important is that the lack of it allows for temptations that lead us away from morality.[8] Kant usually states the first point positively: With happiness, it is easier to be moral. The second point is stated negatively: Without happiness, it is harder to be moral. The first point suggests that there is something positive about the presence of happiness itself that furthers morality. The second point is less forceful than the first, though it is an easier point to argue. It claims that the lack of happiness tempts one to not be moral and so this lack is a hindrance to morality. These then are the two different ways in which happiness can serve as a means to morality. Let me consider these in more detail.

Kant's first claim, that happiness aids in the fulfillment of duty, is stated only in the second *Critique* though there is evidence of it in the *Metaphysics of Morals*. In the second *Critique*, Kant uses the examples of skill, health, and riches to suggest how happiness helps in the carrying out of duty (ibid.). To fill in his argument, it seems to be this: A person with skill, health, and riches finds it easier to be moral because of the presence of his or her skill, health, and riches. Kant does not explain exactly how or why skill, health, and riches lead a person to be moral and similarly he says no more about how happiness facilitates morality.

There are two other places which shed some light on Kant's claim. First, in the *Metaphysics of Morals*, Kant says that "happiness is merely the means of removing the hindrances to morality" (MM,46/6,388). Now it could be argued that happiness is acting in a positive way, by doing something, to help realize morality. Namely, it is removing hindrances to morality. So, this action on the part of happiness is an example of the first reason happiness is important—it aids in the fulfillment of duty—and not of the second—its absence contains temptations. In other words, the presence of happiness (skill, health, and riches) removes obstacles in the way of morality.

Second, when Kant speaks of other indirect duties, quite apart from the duty to pursue personal happiness, he again refers to them as means to morality. For instance, he states that in a person's indirect duties towards animals, animals are means toward the end which is humanity (LE,239/M,302). The performing of indirect duties towards animals helps to "support" and "cultivate" duties toward human beings (ibid.). Similarly, Kant says, the indirect duty to express natural feelings for others serves as a means to feelings based on moral principles (MM,122/6,457).[9] Clearly these passages too suggest that there is a positive way in which the object of an indirect duty furthers or brings about moral ends.

Kant's second claim is that the lack of happiness contains temptations that lead persons away from morality. Happiness thus becomes a means to morality in a negative sense since the absence of happiness leads away from morality. This point is made in almost identical ways in Kant's three major works on ethics. Thus, there is more textual evidence on this point concerning what follows from the absence of happiness than there is for the first point concerning what follows from the presence of happiness.

In the *Groundwork*, the lack of happiness is said to be "a great *temptation to the transgression of duty*" (Gr.67/4,399). In the second *Critique*, the lack of happiness is said to contain "temptations to transgress against duty" (CPR,96/5,93). The *Metaphysics of Morals* reports that the lack of happiness allows for "great temptations to transgress one's duty" and hence that happiness provides "the means of removing the hindrances to morality" (MM,46/6,388). In short, without happiness, it is harder for a person to be moral. If a person lacks happiness, he or she is more likely to be tempted to ignore or to violate duty. Clearly, Kant believes that without happiness a person is less likely to be moral and therefore that happiness is a means to morality.

Kant uses the example of poverty in both the second *Critique* and the *Metaphysics of Morals*. It is easier to be tempted to violate duty if a person is poor than if a person is wealthy. Wealth enables a person to guard against this temptation. Wealth then is a means to a moral end. Wealth is important not because it is itself a moral end but because without it a person is led more easily away from the true moral end.

Kant's example is a simple one and the argument seems to be this. If a person is poor, he or she is more likely to be tempted to steal or harm (to act in a way that fails to realize the moral end). If a person is rich, there is less temptation to steal or harm because there is less lacking to that person. In other words, it becomes easier for the wealthy person to overcome the temptation to steal or harm. (I will not consider here whether or not this is true.) The lack of wealth, or what is really meant, the lack of happiness, prohibits or works against the furtherance of morality.

This is what Kant has to say about happiness insofar as it functions as a means to morality. There are not very many details. In spite of the examples he offers to show that happiness is both an aid to the attainment of morality and that its absence is a hindrance to the attainment of morality, the comprehension of these points is based largely on common sense, not argument.

It is also possible that Kant's two points are really one and the same. Maybe there are not two different tasks happiness performs as a means, but only one that Kant formulates in different ways. Maybe what it is for happiness to facilitate morality is precisely to guard against temptations. Kant's illustration of these two points in terms of riches and poverty seems to lend itself to the view that there is really only one point stated two ways. Riches somehow make it easier to be moral. Poverty, however, makes it easier to be tempted from morality and so, wealth is to be preferred as a way of avoiding temptation, that is, as a way of making easier the path to morality. It sounds like these make the same point. Thus, there may or may not be two separate ways that happiness functions as a means to a moral end. Kant's statement in the second *Critique* specifies these two reasons for why happiness is important as a means, although the other texts do not offer much corroboration. Ultimately, this issue of whether happiness serves as a means in two ways or in one way is not significant to the point at hand. It is sufficient to have established that, for Kant, happiness is a means to morality and to have characterized the way(s) it is such.

II. The Pursuit of Happiness As an Indirect Duty

Let me return to the three texts in order to show the connection between happiness as a means to morality and indirect duties. Again, Kant's claim seems quite clear. Put simply, human beings have an indirect duty to pursue happiness given that happiness is a means to morality. In fact, it appears that whenever some state or object is a means to morality, human beings have an indirect duty to pursue it.

The first passage claims that: "To assure one's own happiness is a duty (at least indirectly)" (Gr.67/4,399). The second states that: "It can even be a duty in certain respects to provide for one's happiness . . . But to further one's happiness can never be a direct duty" (CPR,96/5,93). The third passage says that: "It is not directly a duty to seek affluence for itself [though Kant is really talking about happiness] but indirectly it may very well be a duty" (MM,46/6,388). The notion of indirectness is central to all these passages. They agree that whatever this duty to happiness may entail, it is at best an indirect duty.

Now the question is what is meant here by "indirect." The point seems to be, as suggested above, that the pursuit of happiness is an indirect duty because happiness is the means to morality, not itself the end of morality. Presumably, if the pursuit of personal happiness were a direct duty, then happiness would itself be the end at which the duty aims. Human beings do have direct duties to pursue the happiness of others and their own perfection. But the furthering of personal happiness cannot be a direct duty, since happiness cannot be the end of a will acting from duty. In short, the seeking of happiness becomes an indirect duty only thanks to the relationship of happiness to an end which it facilitates and to which persons have direct duties.

Toward moral or objective ends, a person has direct duties. Toward intermediate states or objects which further moral ends, a person has indirect duties. Human beings thus ought to pursue these intermediate states or objects, not in themselves, but for the sake of what they bring about. These means have some moral value and the pursuit of them becomes a moral duty in a derivative or secondary way, thanks to that at which they aim. Happiness is one of these means that enable persons to better (more quickly? efficiently?) satisfy their direct duties. Kant's idea in general is that the pursuit of certain states or objects becomes required in a secondary sense due to the effect that these states or objects have on a person's ability to realize the direct ends of morality. Happiness is important, and the pursuit of happiness is morally required, because happiness affects the will's ability to achieve its ends.

One point that may be raised concerns Kant's language in describing this duty to seek personal happiness. The three passages use different terms in speaking of the duty to seek happiness. As quoted above, in the order in which Kant wrote them, the relevant claims are:

1. To assure one's own happiness is a duty [*ist Pflicht*] (Gr.67/4,399).
2. It can even be a duty in certain respects to provide for one's happiness [*Es kann sogar in gewissem Betracht Pflicht sein*] (CPR,96/5,93).
3. It is not directly a duty to seek affluence for itself; but indirectly it may very well be a duty [*ist direct nicht Pflicht; aber indirect kann es eine solche wohl sein*] (MM,46/6,388).

Roughly translated, the first text says the pursuit of happiness *is* a duty, the second says it *can be* a duty in certain respects, and the third says it *may very well be* a duty. Both of the latter two claims sound less certain than the first that the seeking of one's own happiness is a duty. There is a difference between identifying the pursuit of personal happiness as a duty and admitting that in some ways it can be or may very well be a duty.[10] To make the best possible case for an indirect duty to pursue happiness, it would have been better if Kant had written the statements in reverse order. In that way it could have been claimed that Kant became convinced over a period of time that the furthering of one's own happiness not only looks like a duty but is a duty. As it stands, a critic might claim the opposite. Maybe Kant became less sure that the pursuit of one's own happiness is a duty since he at least seems less inclined to call it a duty.

However, there is no real reason to reach this conclusion. It is curious that the language in the three statements differs. It may perhaps be a sign that Kant was less inclined in later years to call the seeking of personal happiness a duty. This disinclination may be in part responsible for the almost complete absence of commentary by subsequent readers of Kant on the duty to pursue personal happiness. Or perhaps Kant was simply being more careful and aiming to avoid misinterpretations that might arise in speaking of a duty to further one's own happiness. Nonetheless, there is no definite indication that Kant changed his mind about the indirect duty to pursue personal happiness. What is constant in these texts is Kant's insistence that indirectly human beings have or, taking only the weakest case, they probably have an obligation to seek their own happiness since happiness is a means to morality.

A critic might still ask, how can Kant recognize any duty to pursue personal happiness. Hasn't Kant explicitly ruled this out? For instance, in the *Metaphysics of Morals*, he says: "one's own happiness is an end which . . . can never without contradiction be regarded as a duty" (MM,43/6,386), and "happiness is not an end which is at the same time a duty" (MM,45/6,387). The reason why the end of personal happiness can never be regarded as a duty is that duty involves constraint to an end that is not gladly adopted (MM,43/6,386). Our inclinations are constrained by the moral law and so duty constrains us by determining us to action however reluctantly (CPR,83/5,80). Since all persons do already "gladly adopt" the end of happiness, the notion of a duty to such an end is a contradiction. Given this, how can Kant recognize an indirect duty to pursue personal happiness?

Before answering this question, contrast the above passages with these: "But to further one's happiness can never be a direct duty" (CPR,96/5,93); and "To assure one's own happiness is a duty (at least indirectly)" (Gr.67/4,399). In the *Groundwork*, Kant even refers to "the law of furthering his happiness, not from inclination, but from duty" (ibid.). These passages insist that the pursuit of personal happiness is not a direct duty, but is an indirect duty. The law, duty, can obligate persons to seek their own happiness.

The key is Kant's language. There is no duty to pursue happiness as an end but there is a duty to pursue happiness for the sake of some other moral end. Kant rules out the end of personal happiness as a duty but allows that there is a duty, albeit not direct, to pursue personal happiness. Since duty involves constraint towards an end, there can be no duty to pursue happiness as an end (there is no constraint) but there remains the duty to pursue happiness as a means (towards the end of morality, for which there is constraint). Once the various possible tasks of happiness have been distinguished, it is consistent to say there is no duty to pursue happiness as an end (see chapter 3) but there is a duty to pursue it as a means (this chapter). There is no duty to pursue what we enjoy as an end but there is a duty to pursue it as a means to a moral end. Perhaps to avoid confusion Kant ought not to have called indirect duties "duties" but their inclusion in this category is intelligible given the definition of duty as constraint towards an end and the distinction between ends and means.

There is one further issue to consider. Section I considered Kant's discussion of happiness as a means to morality. It was shown that Kant uses the example of poverty to argue that the lack of happiness makes it harder to be moral while happiness makes it easier to be moral. The point is that when Kant speaks of happiness as a means to a moral end, it is happiness itself, the state of happiness, he is talking about. Passage 2 says "(since it [happiness] includes skill, health, and riches) it contains means to the fulfilment of one's duty" (CPR,96/5,93). Passage 3 says "happiness is merely the means of removing the hindrances to morality" (MM,46/6,388). It is happiness itself, the possession of happiness, that furthers morality.

On the other hand, when Kant is speaking of a person's indirect duties, he is referring to the *pursuit* of happiness and not to the attainment of happiness.[11] Passage 2 claims: "It can even be a duty in certain respects to provide for one's happiness" (CPR,96/5,93). Passage 3 speaks of the "duty to promote one's own happiness" and concludes that: "It is not directly a duty to seek affluence [read: happiness] for itself; but indirectly it may very well be a duty" (MM,46/6,388). Human beings have an indirect duty to seek happiness but not an indirect duty to attain it. They have an indirect duty to pursue happiness although it is the possession of happiness that furthers morality.

This is consistent with Kant's claim in the second *Critique* that people do not have duties that they are not able to carry out, or, as he puts it, whatever a person wills to do, he or she can do. Kant says, "It is always in everyone's power to satisfy the commands of the categorical command of morality" (CPR,38/5,36). Hence, for each person, "whatever he wills to do he also can do" (ibid.,37). Kant states that for the commands of morality, all that is required is a pure maxim while for the precepts of happiness, there is also the question of a person's "capacity and physical ability to realize a desired object" (ibid.). It follows that the indirect duty to pursue happiness can be a duty only to the pursuit of happiness (because that by willing a person can do) and not to the attainment of happiness (because that by willing a person cannot necessarily do). A duty, a moral command, is not concerned with *realizing* a desired object and so the question of a person's *ability to realize* is not an issue.

A person cannot completely control whether or not he or she will achieve happiness. Will he or she possess wealth, strength, health, skill, and so forth? It is in part an empirical question, it is up to Nature, the natural world, whether or not a person will achieve happiness. So it makes no sense to speak of a duty to achieve some object or state whose achievement does not depend entirely on the person. Nevertheless, there may be a duty to pursue such an object or state.[12] A person can will to seek an object or state. That is what Kant is proposing. The pursuit of personal happiness is a duty for persons because the achievement of personal happiness when it comes furthers morality.

III. Other Indirect Duties

There are passages in both the *Lectures on Ethics* and the *Metaphysics of Morals* in which Kant speaks of indirect duties other than the duty to pursue personal happiness. These passages both enumerate other indirect duties and confirm the characterization of what it means to be an indirect duty. These passages confirm that a person has indirect duties toward those things and indirect duties to seek those states that serve as means to morality. They reinforce the claim that there are indirect duties, according to Kant, and that these duties arise as a way of facilitating morality.

These other indirect duties Kant mentions seem to be of three types: duties towards inanimate objects, duties towards animals, and duties towards other beings. In the *Lectures on Ethics*, Kant speaks of the following indirect duties: duties towards inanimate objects, duties towards animals, and duties towards immaterial beings [*Pflichten gegen Sachen, Tiere und andere Wesen*] (the order of the duties is mine, not Kant's) (LE,241/M,304).[13] The *Lectures on Ethics* treats explicitly duties towards lifeless things and animals and the *Metaphysics of Morals* refers to duties to animals and other beings. Given these three types of indirect duties, plus of course the duty to seek personal happiness, it might be concluded that a person has indirect duties towards virtually everything. Probably Kant would not resist this conclusion. It seems possible that almost any object or positive state (excluding those negative states Kant has listed: poverty, ill health, lack of happiness, etc.) might serve to remove a stumbling block to morality or otherwise act as a means to morality.

Kant says in the *Lectures on Ethics*:

> Baumgarten speaks of duties towards inanimate objects. These duties are also indirectly duties towards mankind.[14] Destructiveness is immoral; we ought not to destroy things which can still be put to some use. No man ought to mar the beauty of nature; for what he has no use for may still be of use to some one else. He need, of course, pay no heed to the thing itself, but he ought to consider his neighbor (LE,241/M,304).

Thus, Kant concludes, a person has indirect duties towards inanimate objects such as natural objects (trees, flowers). The real end in a person's treatment of these objects is mankind. As Kant says, a person need pay no heed to the thing itself. The object becomes an object towards which a person has duties due to the effect that the person's treatment of this object has on mankind. Kant does not mention the term "means" here nor does he speak of how our treatment of natural objects is a means to moral ends or how our treatment of natural objects removes hindrances in the way of morality. But his claim that it is not the object of nature which is deserving of attention but mankind, a person's neighbor, is enough to suggest that the indirect duty towards natural objects arises not due to the object but due to that end toward which the object aims. Implicit in this is the notion of means. Kant is more explicit about means, ends, and indirect duties in his discussion of duties towards animals.

Kant says:

> But so far as animals are concerned, we have no direct duties. Animals are not self-conscious and are there merely as a means to an end. That end is man . . . Our duties towards animals are merely indirect duties towards humanity.[15] Animal nature has analogies to human nature, and by doing our duties to animals in respect of manifestations which correspond to manifestations of human nature, we indirectly do our duty towards humanity. Thus, if a dog has served his master long and faithfully, his service, on the analogy of human service, deserves reward, and when the dog has grown too old to serve, his master ought to keep him until he dies. Such action helps to support [*befördere*] us in our duties towards human beings, where they are bounden duties. If then any acts of animals are analogous to human acts and spring from the same principles, we have duties towards the animals because thus we cultivate [*befördern*] the corresponding duties towards human beings (LE,239-40/M,302).

This passage in speaking of a person's indirect duties towards animals makes several claims reminiscent of the discussion of a person's indirect duty to pursue personal happiness. First, there are indirect duties to pursue certain states and to act towards certain objects, here animals, in cases where there are no direct duties to do those things. Second, these indirect duties arise because the state or object is a means to a moral end, namely, humanity. Somehow the object of the indirect duty facilitates or furthers morality.

Here, in Kant's analysis of the indirect duty towards a faithful dog, he says the performance of the indirect duty "supports" and "cultivates" [*befördern*] duties towards human beings. The idea seems to be that by carrying out indirect duties towards animals, a person is encouraged or supported in his or her carrying out of direct duties. This implies that a person who carries out indirect duties is more likely to succeed in carrying out direct duties. Indeed Kant goes on to relate that a person who is cruel to animals is cruel also to people. A child who is cruel to animals becomes an adult who is cruel to children and others (LE,240/M,302-03). Hence, indirect duties arise because our treatment of certain objects (like flowers or dogs) has an effect on our ability to satisfy direct duties and to achieve moral ends. To put it simply, people have a duty to act in a certain way towards objects which are themselves nonmoral (flowers, dogs, happiness) since their relationship to these objects governs indirectly their relationship towards moral objects (humanity, morality). This is an important claim Kant is making because it means that the natural realm is valuable as a means to the moral realm.

In other words, Kant's discussion of indirect duties seems to indicate a significant point of contact between the natural realm and the moral realm. Kant is often accused of offering a two-world system, a dualism. Certainly there are many senses in which his view can be seen to be dualistic: phenomena/noumena, knowledge/belief, science/faith, sensible/intelligible, causality/freedom, natural/moral, and the like. However, at least as important as these dualisms are Kant's attempts to bridge or accommodate these dualisms. In some cases, the dualities seen truly are simply two ways of talking about, two perspectives on, the same thing. In other cases, the members of the dualities complement each other or are logically required by each other. Here in Kant's discussion of indirect duties is the positing of a point of transition between the natural and the moral realms.

Natural objects (dogs, trees) and natural states (happiness) serve as means to morality. That is, people have indirect duties to act in certain ways toward those natural objects and states because such acting helps them to act morally. These indirect duties are in a way precursors to direct duties. People do not mistake their treatment of a dog or their pursuit of their own happiness for morality but they know such actions have an effect on morality. The natural world is elevated to the level of the moral world (at least people have moral duties to it) because it contributes to the moral world. The natural world is not itself "moral" but since human beings have moral duties towards it, it is not simply natural in the sense of outside the realm of morality either. Dogs and happiness are not moral ends but insofar as human beings have moral duties towards those objects and duties to pursue those states, they are objects of moral concern. The natural realm and the moral realm are thus not entirely distinct. Human beings do not have duties solely to pursue moral ends. The concept of moral obligation applies to natural objects since natural objects help produce or hinder morality.

Put concretely, Kant seems to be saying that a person's ability to be moral is affected by whether or not the person is happy. How we treat our dogs will affect how we treat others and hence will affect our ability to be moral. Hence, our happiness and our dogs are legitimate moral concerns, not because of themselves, but because of what they effect. A person has duties towards natural objects and states; moral duties, since these natural objects and states have an inevitable impact on morality. Thus, Kant's notion of indirect duties makes explicit a connection between the natural and the moral realms. The failure to recognize Kant's notion of indirect duties does serious harm to the understanding of the relationship between the natural and the moral realms.

To return to Kant's description of other indirect duties, consider the *Metaphysics of Morals* where Kant speaks again of the destruction of beautiful though lifeless things in nature. Although he does not explicitly state that people have an indirect duty to these inanimate objects, he does say that such destruction "weakens or destroys that feeling in man which is indeed not of itself already moral, but which still does much to promote [*befördert*] a state of sensibility favorable to morals, or at least to prepare for [*vorbereitet*] such a state" (MM,106/6,443). Thus, again, a person's treatment of natural objects is seen to have an effect on the achievement of morality.

Kant mentions in more direct terms a person's indirect duties to animals and to others. He says:

> Even gratitude for the long-performed service of an old horse or dog (just as if they were members of the household) belongs indirectly to a man's duty [*gehört indirect zur Pflicht des Menschen*], namely, his duty *regarding* these animals; but directly considered, such a duty is always only his duty *to* himself (MM,106/6,443).

> To this end it accordingly is an indirect duty [*indirecte Pflicht*] to cultivate [*cultiviren*] our natural (sensitive) feelings for others, and to make use of them as so many means [*Mittel*] for sympathy based on moral principles and the feeling appropriate to them. Thus it is a duty not to avoid places where the poor, who lack the most necessary things, are to be found; instead it is a duty to seek them out (MM,122/6,457).

Here Kant is discussing two illustrations he has considered before. The first example is the faithful dog. Towards this dog a person has an indirect duty not because of what the dog is in itself but because of the dog's role as a means to the end of humanity. The second example concerns poverty or, in this case, the poor. Earlier Kant uses the example of poverty and wealth to argue that happiness is a means to morality. Here Kant is not considering the state of poverty but the poor and a person's relationship and feelings towards them. He says that a person's natural feelings towards the poor are the means for feelings based on moral principles. Thus, people have an indirect duty to foster these natural feelings towards the poor, in fact, to seek out the places where the poor are to be found in order that moral feelings might be generated.

There are two questions that might be asked about indirect duties. First, it seems that in the last passage quoted above Kant is talking about *feelings* and not about *actions* directed toward a natural object or state. The other texts concern how to treat inanimate objects or animals. They have to do with certain actions that become obligatory for human beings. Thus human beings have indirect duties not to wantonly destroy a natural object and to care for a faithful dog. This last passage is different in that it concerns the cultivating of a feeling.

In a way, it is different but in another way, it is not. Other passages tell people to pursue their own happiness and to act in certain ways towards inanimate objects and animals. These seem to not directly involve their feelings. But the explicit mention of feelings in this passage does not mean Kant is talking about something totally different or that this indirect duty eschews action. Kant's treatment of the poor includes not only the duty to foster natural feelings towards the poor but the duty to seek out those places where the poor are. Thus, the duty is not simply to encourage certain feelings towards others but also to undertake certain actions towards them. In addition, Kant's discussion of the duty to the dog can be formulated as a duty to encourage a certain feeling. He speaks after all about gratitude towards the dog. He says that the destruction of inanimate objects has an effect on that feeling in human beings which serves to promote morality. So here too the indirect duty involves the protection or cultivation of a feeling.

Second, it seems that there may be a difference between the way happiness is a means to morality and the way natural objects, animals, and a person's feelings towards others are means to morality. The reason human beings have an indirect duty to pursue happiness seems to be somewhat different from the reason they have these other indirect duties. These other indirect duties appear to arise in large part for pedagogical reasons. It helps people learn how to treat moral ends if they first learn how to treat inanimate nature and animals. It helps people learn moral feelings if they first cultivate natural feelings. Kant says animal nature has analogies to human nature and that seems to be the crucial point. Because natural objects have analogies to moral objects, our feelings and actions towards natural objects can aid in developing the correct feelings and actions towards moral objects. There is a sense of progression in Kant's talk of how these indirect duties lead to morality. He speaks of these indirect duties as "supporting [*befördere*]," "cultivating [*befördern*]," "promoting [*befördert*]," and "preparing for [*vorbereitet*]" direct duties towards moral ends, that is, morality.

The indirect duty to pursue personal happiness does not however have this same pedagogical result. It is not by possessing personal happiness that human beings learn by analogy what their moral duties are. They do not pursue happiness so that by analogy they will learn how to pursue moral ends. Recall that part of Kant's claim about happiness as a means to morality is a negative claim. Without happiness, it is harder to be moral. Happiness appears to be at least in part a negative condition a person must satisfy in order to have a better chance at morality. Because the lack of happiness can hold a person back from morality, he or she has a derivative, indirect duty to pursue happiness. The point is that the pursuit of happiness does not promote or prepare people for their moral duties in the same way that these other indirect duties do. A person's treatment of lifeless nature, animals, and others seems to lead in a smooth, progressive, analogous fashion to his or her direct duties. The pursuit of happiness does not.

But all the same, it is obvious that there are overwhelming similarities between Kant's talk of these other indirect duties and his talk of the indirect duty to pursue personal happiness. Because morality or humanity is furthered by a thing, human beings have an indirect duty to pursue or to do that thing, whether the "thing" is a state (happiness), an action (treatment of natural objects and animals), or a feeling (gratitude, sympathy). In all these cases, a part of the natural world (state, object, or feeling) becomes the object of a moral duty due to its tendency to facilitate the moral realm. A natural state or object or feeling is validated because it is seen to result in morality.

In the *Metaphysics of Morals*, Kant offers a formal classification of duties which raises questions about this analysis of indirect duties. First, there are duties of human beings to human beings [*des Menschen gegen den Menschen*]. These include duties of human beings to themselves [*gegen sich selbst*] and of human beings to other human beings [*gegen andere Wesen*]. Second, there are duties of human beings to beings which are not human [*des Menschen gegen nicht menschliche Wesen*]. These include duties of human beings to subhuman beings [*untermenschliche Wesen*] and of human beings to superhuman beings [*übermenschliche Wesen*] (MM,73/6,413).

Assuming that this list of duties is complete, the question arises as to how this discussion of indirect duties fits with Kant's scheme. There are two difficulties. First, as shown above, one instance of an indirect duty that Kant discusses is a person's duty towards inanimate objects [*den Pflichten gegen leblose Sachen*] (LE,241/M,304). In his discussion of a person's treatment of things [*Sachen*] and the beauty of nature, Kant seems to admit that people have indirect duties towards natural objects.

Unfortunately, the claim that a person has indirect duties towards natural objects does not fit well with the classification of duties in the *Metaphysics of Morals*.

When classifying duties, Kant speaks only of two types of duties; duties to human beings and duties to nonhuman beings. The only possibility of locating the indirect duty to natural objects within this scheme is to place it under duties of human beings to nonhuman beings, that is, to subhuman beings. Natural objects are certainly not human beings or superhuman beings. However, the categorizing of duties to things [*Sachen*] under the heading of duties to nonhuman beings [*nicht menschliche Wesen*] seems forced and extremely unlikely. Rather than forcing the duty to natural objects into this scheme of duties, let me allow the discrepancy to stand. Perhaps Kant forgot to include the duty to natural objects in this scheme of duties. Perhaps he considered this duty to natural objects such an insignificant duty that he left it off his formal classification of duties. Perhaps in discussing the duty to natural objects Kant was still operating under the influence of Baumgarten's ethic and by the time he wrote his *Metaphysics of Morals* almost twenty years later he no longer believed human beings have a duty to natural objects. Maybe the students who left us Kant's *Lectures on Ethics* and Kant's treatment of the duty to natural objects simply got it wrong. In any case, there is this gap. The duty to natural objects is not listed in the scheme of duties presented in the *Metaphysics of Morals*.

Second, there is some inconsistency in the language Kant uses to describe a person's indirect duties. Until now, the discussion has been about indirect duties *towards* or *to* natural objects, animals, and others, although in one of the passages quoted earlier Kant makes a distinction between duties regarding and duties to (see page 107). This deserves further consideration.

In the *Metaphysics of Morals*, Kant distinguishes between duties regarding (in regard to) and duties to. He claims that a person confuses "his duty *regarding* other beings with a duty *toward* these beings" (MM,105/6,442).[16] Similarly, when considering the duty to a faithful horse or dog, he says that gratitude is an indirect duty "namely, his duty *regarding* these animals, but directly considered, such a duty is always only his duty *to* himself" (MM,106/6,443).[17] He adds that, "man has no duties except *to* men" (MM,105/6,442; emphasis mine).[18] So, any duty to must be to a person. So-called duties to natural objects, animals, or other nonhuman beings are in fact only duties regarding these objects. These duties regarding objects, animals, and nonhuman beings are actually duties to human beings or humanity. This distinction, if Kant had only used it consistently, could contribute significantly to the understanding of indirect duties.

All duties to are to persons. So any duty about an object, animal, or nonhuman being is a duty regarding that thing. The only complication seems to be whether or not a person could have a duty regarding another human being. There is some unclarity in the use of the term "other beings" [*andere Wesen*] but it appears that the answer is yes, people can have duties regarding other human beings. The unclarity is this. In the chart of duties in the *Metaphysics of Morals*, a person's duty to other beings [*andere Wesen*] is translated as a duty to other human beings (MM,73/6,413). It is one type of a human being's duty to human beings. On the other hand, in the *Lectures on Ethics*, a person's duty to other beings [*andere Wesen*] is translated as a duty to immaterial beings (LE,241/M,304). This duty towards immaterial beings is linked with duties towards animals and things and appears under the heading of "Duties towards lifeless things." In this case, other beings seems to refer not to other human beings. Hence, it is not always clear whether Kant is using the term other beings to refer to human or nonhuman beings.

However, the reason for concluding that human beings may have duties regarding human beings is based on the passages from the *Metaphysics of Morals*. There Kant says that gratitude toward the horse or dog belongs to a human being's duty regarding these animals. The passage quoted next seems to follow the same pattern. It says that cultivating natural feelings towards others belongs to a human being's duty, and here I add the rest, regarding those others. In both cases, it is the feeling and the consequent action that is a person's duty although that toward which the feeling is directed is a dog or a person, as the case may be. The object of a person's action is not directly the dog or the person but the feeling and the action. Hence, the duty requires a person to feel and to do regarding some animal or being because of the value of that feeling and action to morality. Thus, there is no reason to preclude the possibility of duties regarding other persons and in addition there is some evidence to suggest there are such duties.

Unfortunately, Kant does not consistently use his distinction between duties to and duties regarding. In his chart of the duties in the *Metaphysics of Morals*, Kant refers to duties of human beings to beings which are not human (subhuman beings, superhuman beings) (MM,73/6,413). These duties should according to his own distinction be called duties regarding such beings. Also in the *Lectures on Ethics*, Kant speaks of "duties towards inanimate objects [*Pflichten gegen leblose Sachen*]" (LE,241/M,304), "duties towards animals, towards immaterial beings and towards inanimate objects [*Pflichten gegen Tiere, andere Wesen und Sachen*]" (ibid.), and "duties towards the animals [*Pflichten gegen die Tiere*]" (LE,240/M,302). All of these duties are more exactly duties regarding such objects. Thus, it is clear that Kant does not always call these indirect duties "duties regarding" a thing or being and so this unclarity compromises the understanding of his notion of indirect duties.

However, the notion of indirect duties is crucial to an understanding of Kant's ethics. First, it reveals something about the place of happiness in Kant's ethics. Human beings have or, at the very least, probably have an indirect duty to pursue their own happiness. This fact grants to happiness a place in ethics it does not have if it is considered only as a natural end. Happiness is valuable in Kant's ethics because it brings about morality. Second, the notion of indirect duties reveals something about the extent of a human being's duties. People have a whole series of duties to natural objects and animals that may not be obvious in Kant's talk of duty for duty's sake or in his talk of treating people as ends in themselves, not simply as means. Third, the notion of indirect duties points to a connection between the natural realm and the moral realm. The notion of an indirect duty bridges the gap between the natural and the moral realms by recognizing that the natural realm is a means to the moral realm. The natural realm facilitates or helps bring about the moral realm. Here, in the notion of the indirect duty, is one place Kant posits a connection between nonmoral objects and moral ends. Kant is serious about the notion of indirect duties and since the pursuit of personal happiness is identified as such a duty, it follows that happiness as a means is good and its pursuit is a duty.

Chapter Five

The Positive Role of Happiness As Part of a Moral End (the Highest Good)

This is the last part of Kant's treatment of happiness, following his analysis of the role of happiness as a principle for action, as a natural end, and as a means to a moral end. There remains Kant's discussion of happiness insofar as it forms part of the highest good. The highest good, a moral end, indeed the highest moral end, contains happiness as one of its components. Since happiness is *in* the highest good, the investigation of the role of happiness in ethics must consider the role of the highest good in ethics.

There has been considerable debate over the last thirty years (especially among English-speaking Kant critics) concerning the import of Kant's doctrine of the highest good. No one denies Kant has a notion of the highest good and that he believes it to be important to his ethics. The discussion concerns whether or not it is *really* important or necessary to his ethics and, if so, *why* exactly it is important. This debate is known as the Beck-Silber controversy. L. W. Beck apparently was the first to argue that for Kant's ethics the highest good is unimportant and John Silber was the first to defend its importance. By now many more have entered the debate. My intent here is not primarily to contribute to this debate although I discuss these issues and reach certain conclusions regarding them. My goal is to illuminate the role of happiness in Kant's ethics and to do this it is necessary to consider happiness in its role as part of the highest good. I am first of all interested in happiness but in this chapter by way of the highest good.

Many of the participants in the debate over the importance of the highest good are considered in what follows. The controversy is no longer simply over whether the highest good is important or unimportant to Kant's ethics. The concern now is with questions like the following. Is the highest good a determining ground of the will? Is it content for the will? Is its pursuit a duty? If so, what kind of a duty is it? Does the highest good have important practical consequences? These are some of the issues to be considered in what follows.

Section I discusses Kant's definition of the highest good. It is shown that happiness is a part of the highest good. Section II looks at the initial descriptions Kant gives of the roles of the highest good. Section III deals with the issues raised by commentators, among them, Beck and Silber, concerning the importance of the highest good.

I. Definition of the Highest Good

In order to consider Kant's descriptions of what the highest good is, the most important text by far is the second *Critique*. It is there in the Dialectic section that Kant considers systematically and in some detail the concept of the highest good. In fact, a good argument can be made that the central topic of the Dialectic is the highest good, plus those topics raised by the highest good. However, that aside, this section considers primarily the second *Critique*, and those more minor references to the highest good which occur in the *Lectures on Ethics*, *Critique of Pure Reason*, *Theory and Practice*, *Religion Within the Limits of Reason Alone*, and *Critique of Judgment*.

What is the highest good? Kant's answer in a sentence is: happiness in proportion to worth.[1] The highest good is that combination of happiness and virtue in which happiness is awarded in proportion to virtuousness or moral worth. The *Lectures on Ethics* claims: "In mankind therefore we have to look both for happiness [*Glückseligkeit*] and for merit [*Würdigkeit*]. The combination of the two will be the highest good [*das höchste Gut*]" (LE,6/M,7). The first *Critique* asserts: "Happiness [*Glückseligkeit*], therefore, in exact proportion with the morality [*Sittlichkeit*] of the rational beings who are thereby rendered worthy [*würdig sind*] of it, alone constitutes the highest good [*das höchste Gut*]" (A814/B842).[2] Thus, the highest good is defined as that combination, that proportionality, between happiness and moral worth. There seems to be no question but that happiness is one of the two components of the highest good, such that when we talk about the highest good, we are talking in part about happiness.

In the second *Critique*, the highest good is described in these ways. Kant says: "virtue [*Tugend*] and happiness [*Glückseligkeit*] together constitute the possession of the highest good [*des höchsten Guts*] for one person, and happiness [*Glückseligkeit*] in exact proportion to morality [*Sittlichkeit*] . . . constitutes that of a possible world" (CPR,115/5,110). Kant goes on to call morality [*Sittlichkeit*] the first condition [*erste Bedingung*] of the highest good [*des höchsten Guts*] and happiness [*Glückseligkeit*] the second element [*zweite Element*] of the highest good (CPR,123/5,119). Later, the first and principal part of the highest good [*des höchsten Guts*] is said to be morality [*Sittlichkeit*] while the second element of the highest good is happiness in proportion to morality [*der jener Sittlichkeit angemessenen Glückseligkeit*] (CPR,128-29/5,124). Finally, in reference to the Stoics, Kant asserts that "they really left out of the highest good the second element (personal happiness) [*das zweite Element des höchsten Guts, eigene Glückseligkeit*]" (CPR,132/5,127). Thus, the highest good is made up in part by virtue (or morality or worth) and in part by happiness.

Similarly, in *Theory and Practice*, Kant says that the human will must strive as best it can "for the *highest good* that is possible in the world (universal happiness linked to and in accordance with the purest morality in the world as a whole)" (TP,46/8,279).[3] The *Religion* describes the highest good in a similar way. It refers to "(happiness proportioned to obedience to duty)—that is to say, the idea of a highest good in the world" (Rel.4/6,5).[4] Here too virtue and happiness together are said to make up the highest good.

Now, not all of these descriptions of the highest good are identical. For instance, some of the passages speak of the combination of virtue and happiness, others speak more specifically of a proportionality between virtue and happiness. Some refer to personal happiness while others refer to universal happiness. Some distinguish between the highest good for one person and the highest good for the world; others do not. Some passages describe the highest good in the world; others are not so specific. So, it is obvious that these passages do not provide perfectly identical definitions of the highest good. However, what is important first is the similarity in these definitions. Namely, the highest good is identified consistently by Kant as the combination of virtue and happiness. Happiness is a part, the second part, of the object Kant calls "the highest good." The dissimilarities in the definitions of the highest good are treated later in this chapter and in chapter 6.

Next, there are two objects which are called the highest good in the *Groundwork*, though neither is that combination of virtue and happiness so far identified with the highest good. Kant calls both the good will and God the highest good. These identifications it seems are simply not exact. These objects cannot really be identified with the highest good and Kant clarifies in the second *Critique* and other places the extent to which the good will and God may be equivalent to the highest good. The problem is how to deal with two passages in which the good will and God are said to be the highest good. Neither is the same as "happiness in accordance with morality." The solution is to look at other passages in which Kant qualifies and modifies his identification of the good will and God with the highest good.

The first passage, dealing with the functions of reason, claims that the good will is the highest good:

> Its [reason's] true function must be to produce a *will* which is *good* . . . Such a will need not on this account be the sole and complete good, but it must be the highest good and the condition of all the rest, even of all our demands for happiness (Gr.64/4,396).[5]

According to this, a good will is the highest good (*das höchste Gut*), the condition of all the rest, though it need not be the sole (*einzige*) or complete (*ganze*) good. How can this claim be reconciled with Kant's earlier definition of the highest good as happiness in proportion to worth?

Kant provides the answer himself in the second *Critique*. By explaining an ambiguity in the meaning of "highest," he shows that while "highest good" can mean the condition of all the rest, in its fullest sense, in the way in which Kant goes on to use the term, highest good means the entire, the whole, the perfect good. Thus, it is because there is an ambiguity in the meaning of highest that a good will and happiness in accordance with morality are both called the highest good.

Kant makes these claims:

> The concept of the "highest" contains an ambiguity . . . The "highest" [*das höchste*] can mean the "supreme" (*supremum*) [*das Oberste*] or the "perfect" (*consummatum*) [*das Vollendete*]. The former is the unconditional condition, i.e., the condition which is subordinate to no other (*originarium*); the latter is that whole which is no part of a yet larger whole of the same kind (*perfectissimum*). That virtue [*Tugend*] (as the worthiness to be happy) is the supreme condition [*die oberste Bedingung*] of whatever appears to us to be desir-

> able and thus of all our pursuit of happiness and, consequently, that it is the supreme good [*das oberste Gut*] have been proved in the Analytic. But these truths do not imply that virtue is the entire and perfect good [*das ganze und vollendete Gut*] . . . For this, happiness is also required . . . Inasmuch as virtue and happiness together constitute the possession of the highest good [*des höchsten Guts*] for one person, . . . the highest good means the whole, the perfect good [*das Ganze, das vollendete Gute*], wherein virtue is always the supreme good [*das oberste Gut*], being the condition having no condition superior to it (CPR,114-15/5,110-11).
>
> The supreme good (as the first condition of the highest good) is morality (CPR,123/5,119).[6]

The point of these passages is that Kant qualifies the meaning of highest good. Highest can mean "supreme," that is, first, unconditional condition, and it can mean "perfect," that is, the entire, the whole not part of a larger whole. Kant here assigns the term "supreme good" to the former and highest good to the latter. Thus, the supreme good, the unconditioned condition, is virtue or morality or, from the earlier passage, the good will. The highest good, the entire, the perfect whole, is happiness in accord with virtue. The passage from the *Groundwork* labels a good will not the sole and complete good but the condition of all the rest, that is, the highest good. But Kant insists in the second *Critique* that that which is not the entire and perfect good but is the condition subordinate to no other is better called "the supreme good."[7] Even though the term highest can be used in one sense to apply to virtue, morality, a good will, the point of Kant's clarification of the term highest is to restrict its use to virtue and happiness together. Hence, the claim in the *Groundwork* is not wrong when it calls a good will the highest good but it is inexact and certainly misleading given the way Kant generally restricts the term highest good to its other meaning.

Therefore, in light of the second *Critique*, this claim can be amended to read: "Such a will [a good will] . . . must be the *supreme* good and the condition of all the rest, even of all our demands for happiness."

The second passage claims that God is the highest good or at least acknowledges that human beings have the idea of God as the highest good. The text considers why morality cannot be derived from examples and asks: "Where do we get the concept of God as the highest good?" (Gr.76/4,408-09).[8] The answer is that it comes from the Idea of moral perfection, that is, from reason. The problem arises because a reader might infer from this passage that God is being identified with the highest good. If God is now considered to be the highest good, what happens to the earlier definition of the highest good as happiness in proportion to worth?

The answer again is provided by Kant himself. In several texts, especially the second *Critique*, Kant takes pains to qualify the sense in which God is the highest good and to distinguish this notion of the highest good from that which is equivalent to happiness in proportion to worth. The passage in the *Groundwork* is not exactly wrong to have spoken of God as the highest good but it is misleading. Given what Kant says in other places, there is no reason why both God and happiness in proportion to worth cannot be called the highest good as long as the reader recalls that the highest good can be understood in two senses.

The point is this. It is possible to distinguish between a highest original good, that is, God, and a highest derived good, that is, happiness in accordance with morality. God retains in a sense the role of highest good while happiness in proportion to worth is posited as the highest good, that is, the end or object of moral agents. For practical purposes, it is this latter highest good which is of particular interest to Kant and of special concern to ethics.

This distinction between senses of the highest good is made explicit in the following places. The *Lectures on*

Ethics defines the highest *created* good as the most perfect world, a world in which rational beings are happy and worthy of happiness (LE,6/M,7).[9] The *Critique of Pure Reason* speaks of God as the highest *original* good [*des höchsten ursprünglichen Guts*] (A810/B838) and of the two elements, happiness and worth, of the highest *derivative* good [*des höchsten abgeleiteten Guts*] (A811/B839). The *Critique of Judgment* specifies that the highest good which is mankind's final purpose, that is, happiness in accordance with worth, is the highest *physical* good (CJ,301/5,450).[10] Thus, in these places, happiness in proportion to worth is identified as the highest created, derivative, and physical good and is contrasted to God as the highest original (presumably, uncreated and nonphysical) good.

Finally, in the second *Critique*, this distinction is made use of again and there is a suggestion regarding how these two notions of the highest good are related. The text is: "the postulate of the possibility of a highest derived good (the best world) is at the same time the postulate of the reality of a highest original good, namely, the existence of God" (CPR,130/5,125).[11] The holy Author of the world "makes possible the derived highest good" (CPR,133/5,128).[12] The passage also speaks of "the holiness of His [God's] will as the highest original good" (CPR,135/5,131)[13] and of "the highest independent good, i.e., the existence of God" (CPR,137/5,132).[14]

What is important about these passages for the aims of this work is that they recognize that the highest good can refer to an original or to a derivative good. Kant can call God the highest good in the *Groundwork* and elsewhere without contradicting himself, even though he usually means by the highest good happiness in proportion to worth. Kant fails to use this distinction much of the time although usually without any indication that he is speaking of the highest original good, the highest good means happiness in proportion to worth.

What is *not* important about these passages for my purposes but is perhaps deserving of further attention are the following points. First, the description of the relationship between the two highest goods is intriguing. The text says both that to postulate the highest derived good is to postulate the highest original good and that the highest original good makes possible the highest derived good. More could be said about this relationship in which the highest derived good implies the highest original good and is made possible by it. Second, the passages identify the highest original good with both the existence of God and with the holiness of God's will. Further, the existence of God is spoken of both as *Existenz* and as *Dasein*. There is room for clarification on these issues.

However, in sum, the highest good which is the object or end of ethics is technically a highest derived, created, physical good. It is also possible to speak of God as the highest good but this time as a highest original, independent good who is not as such the object or end of ethics. Although both a good will and God are called the highest good, neither is equated with the highest good, the object of ethics.[15]

II. Roles of the Highest Good

The highest good, virtue and happiness together, plays several roles in Kant's ethics. Much of the disagreement over the importance of the highest good is due to unclarity in the roles Kant assigns to the highest good.[16] In fact, four tasks for the highest good are specified, tasks which are not mutually exclusive or contradictory. Most generally, the highest good is said to be the *end*, *object*, or *goal* of pure, practical reason, that is, of the will. More specifically, the highest good can be called the *final end*, the *ultimate end*. In its role as end, or final end, the highest good can function as an end for one person (as an *individual end*) and/or as an end for all, for the world (as a *social end*). In other words, the highest good may be thought of as a goal to be achieved by a particular person (a time or a place in which personal happiness is awarded in accord with morality) or as a goal to be achieved for the world, universally (a state to be brought about in which the happiness of all is awarded in accordance with morality).

The argument here is that the highest good serves in these four capacities—as end or object, as final or ultimate end, as individual end, as social end—and that there is no obvious contradiction among these roles.

First is the claim that the highest good is the end, object, or goal of pure practical reason.[17] In the *Critique of Practical Reason* all these terms are used. It says: "the highest good [*das höchste Gut*] is the necessary highest end [*Zweck*] of a morally determined will and a true object [*Object*] thereof" (CPR,119/5,115). It then speaks of "the possibility of the highest good [*des höchsten Guts*] which reason presents to all rational beings as the goal [*Ziels*] of all their moral wishes" (ibid.). Repeatedly in the second *Critique* the highest good is called "the object [*des Gegenstandes*] of the pure practical reason" (CPR,112/5,108), "an a priori necessary object [*Object*] of our will" (CPR,118/5,114), and "the entire object [*Object*] of pure practical reason" (CPR,123/5,119).[18] In *Religion*, it is claimed that the idea of the highest good "cannot be realized by man himself . . . yet he discovers within himself the duty to work for this end [*Zweck*]" (Rel.130/6,139).

There are also passages in which this task of the highest good as end or object is linked to its second task as final end. The second *Critique* speaks of "the concept of the highest good as the object [*Object*] and final end [*Endzweck*] of pure practical reason" (CPR,134/5,129). Similarly, it states in *Theory and Practice* that the concept of duty "*introduced* another end [*Zweck*] for the human will: namely, to strive as best he can for the *highest good*" (TP,46/8,279) and then the footnote on this page asserts that the highest good is "the moral *ultimate end* [*als moralischer Endzweck*]" (TP,46n/8,279). The highest good is identified as "the ultimate end [*letzten Zweck*] of a will" (TP,47/8,280).

Hence, the second task assigned to the highest good is that of final or ultimate end.[19] There is further evidence of this role of the highest good in the second *Critique*, the third *Critique*, and *Religion*. For example: "The moral law commands us to make the highest possible good in a world the final object [*letzten Gegenstande*] of all our conduct" (CPR,134/5,129). In *Religion*, it is said that the idea of a highest good in the world meets "our natural need to conceive of some sort of final end [*Endzweck*] for all our actions" (Rel.5/6,5). A later passage reads: "Make the highest good possible in the world your own final end [*Endzweck*!] is a synthetic proposition *a priori*" (Rel.7n/6,7).[20]

The third *Critique* offers similar evidence of the role of the highest good as final end although the account is more complex. The *Critique* notes that human beings propose to themselves "as highest purpose [*als höchsten Zweck*] (the highest good [*höchste Gut*] in the world)" (CJ,285/5,435). The moral law determines for us "a final purpose [*Endzweck*] toward which it obliges us to strive and this purpose is the *highest good* [*höchste Gut*] *in the world*" (CJ,301/5,450). Thus, the final purpose [*Endzweck*] of all rational beings is said to be happiness insofar as it is possible for it to accord with duty (CJ,323n/5,471n).

While the third *Critique* reiterates the role of the highest good as final or ultimate end, it also applies the term final end to man. Repeatedly, in the section on the methodology of teleological judgment, it is stated that: "man is the final purpose [*Endzweck*] of creation" (CJ,286/5,435), man is "the ultimate purpose [*letzten Zweck*] of nature" (CJ,279/5,429), and "it is only as a moral being that man can be a final purpose [*Endzweck*] of creation" (CJ,294/5,443). Still, it is quite evident that human beings are not final ends in the same way that the highest good is a final end. Humanity is the ultimate end of nature, understood as the unconditioned end to which all the conditioned ends of nature are subordinate. Thanks to humanity, the purposive arrangements we recognize in nature have an unconditioned ground. On the other hand, the moral law or reason prescribes for humanity an object as final end. The final end of pure practical reason is that which humanity (the final end of creation) is constrained to strive for, namely, the highest good.

There is much more which needs to be said about the role of these two final ends with regard to teleological judgment and about the relationship between these two final ends, but since that is not our concern here, I note only this. The relationship between these two final ends is complex and intriguing. There is a sense in which the final end of creation seems dependent on the final end of reason and vice versa, a way that the final end of reason seems to depend on that of creation. It is only as noumenon, as subject of morality, that humanity is the final end of creation (CJ,285-86/5,435). It is only by working out the final end of reason that humanity becomes worthy of being the final end of creation (CJ,322/5,469). On the other hand, it is because the moral law requires us to aim at an ultimate end that we have ground for thinking a final end of creation (CJ,306/5,455). Once the relationship is described this way: If the final end of rational beings is to be objectively real then creation must have a final end; and if creation has a final end, it must harmonize with the moral end (CJ,304/5,453). The final ends of creation and reason though different are related. Humanity as the ultimate end of nature is already not a natural end in that it is humanity as noumenon at issue. Clearly, the third *Critique* uses the notion of final end in a broader way by applying it to creation although still the task of the highest good as final end of reason is evident.

Now, the question is, what does it mean for the highest good to be a final end. In *Theory and Practice* and in *Religion* there are quite similar accounts of what it is to be a final end. Both assert that a final end is one which is composed of the entirety or sum of all the ends of moral conduct. *Theory and Practice* considers the "ultimate end established by pure reason and comprising the entirety of all ends under one principle" (TP,47n/8,280). In *Religion*, it is said: "The end which embraces the unavoidable and at the same time sufficient condition of all other ends is the *final end* [*Endzweck*]" (Rel.6n/6,6). It is claimed that "the concept of a final end [*Endzweck*] of all things . . . while not multiplying men's duties, yet provides them with a special point of focus for the unification of all ends" (Rel.5/6,5). So, the final end is not an additional end which the pure will must adopt on top of all of its other ends (for instance, the happiness of others, one's own perfection, etc.). Rather, the final end is the unification of all ends and hence in willing the final end a moral agent is in essence willing all other moral ends at once.[21]

So far then, the highest good has been said to be both end or object of the will and final end or object of the will. Is there any inconsistency in the assignment of these two roles to the highest good? The answer is "no." The highest good is the end or object of the will though this fact does not mean it cannot be the final end of the will. In the same way, being the final end of the will does not make the highest good not the end or object of the will. Its role as end of the will does not preclude its role as final end of the will and its role as final end does not invalidate its role as end. These two tasks of the highest good can peacefully co-exist.

Finally, an important issue follows from the recognition that the highest good is the end, the final end, of the pure will. Chapter 3 argued that ends are always determining grounds of the will though objective or moral ends are not the only determining ground of the pure will. These moral ends dictated by pure practical reason work together with the form of the moral law to determine the will. So the ends themselves do not determine the will (if they do, heteronomy results) but in conjunction with the form of the law, objective ends act to determine the will to action. Hence, insofar as something is an end, it is a determining ground of the will.

Now, since the highest good has been seen to be the end, the final end, of the pure will, it would seem to follow that the highest good is a determining ground of the will. Based on earlier arguments, this conclusion is inevitable. The highest good must then act in conjunction with the form of the moral law to determine the will to act. This issue of whether or not the highest good is a determining ground of the will is one treated by commentators involved in the debate over the importance of the highest good. This issue is reconsidered in section III.

Finally, the last two tasks assigned to the highest good specify the type of end or final end which the highest good is. On the one hand, the highest good is said to be an individual end, that is, the goal of an individual person who aims to have personal happiness awarded in accordance with personal worth. On the other hand, the highest good is a social end, a world to be brought about, in which the happiness of all is awarded in accordance with the worth of all. Thus, the highest good may be a goal for individuals or a goal for the world or, assuming these are not mutually exclusive, a goal for both.[22]

The clearest statement of these two tasks of the highest good comes from the second *Critique*:

> Virtue and happiness together constitute the possession of the highest good for one person [*des höchsten Guts in einer Person*], and happiness in exact proportion to morality (as the worth of a person and his worthiness to be happy) constitutes that of a possible world [*das höchste Gut einer möglichen Welt*] (CPR,115/5,110).

What is significant is that this passage distinguishes between the highest good for one person and the highest good of a possible world. It must therefore be possible to distinguish between the highest good for one person, as individual end, and the highest good of a world, as social end.

Unfortunately, there is not much textual evidence for the role of the highest good as individual end. Aside from this one passage in the second *Critique*, there is no explicit statement about the highest good for one person. Instead, there are many passages that refer to the highest good of the world or in the world and many more passages which are not specific and simply speak of the highest good. Thus, though it is stated that the highest good can be understood to mean "in a person" (for one), the focus is on the highest good "in a world" (for all).

The strongest claims about the social nature of the highest good as end are found in *Religion*. That work states that: "the species of rational beings is objectively . . . destined for a social goal, namely, the promotion of the highest as a social good" (Rel.89/6,97). Furthermore, it refers to "the world's highest good" (Rel.161/6,173) and concedes that "it is a duty of a peculiar kind (*officium sui generis*) to unite oneself with an ethical commonwealth" (Rel.139/6,151).

Other texts lend support to this view of the highest good as social end. *Theory and Practice* refers to "the *highest good* that is possible in the world (universal happiness linked to and in accordance with the purest morality in the world as a whole)" (TP,46/8,279). The *Lectures on Ethics* adds: "The highest created good is the most perfect world, that is, a world in which all rational beings are happy and are worthy of happiness" (LE,6/M,7).[23] The second *Critique* repeatedly speaks of "the achievement of the highest good in the world" (CPR,126/5,122), "a highest derived good (the best world) [*der besten Welt*]" (CPR,130/5,125), and "the highest possible good in a world" (CPR,134/5,129).

It is even clearer that the highest good is understood to be a social end in those texts that speak of reason's final or ultimate end. Since the highest good is our final end, any description of the final end as a world applies as well to the highest good. For instance, *Theory and Practice* considers the ultimate end [*Endzweck*] to be "a world [*eine Welt*] as the highest good possible through our collaboration" (TP,47n/8,280). *Perpetual Peace* maintains that the objective final end [*Endzweck*] of the human race is perpetual peace, a state of affairs in the world (PP,106/8,361). The *Critique of Judgment* speaks of our final purpose [*Endzweck*] as the highest good [*höchsten Weltbesten*], the *summum bonum* [*Weltbeste*] which is universal happiness conjoined with morality (CJ,302,304/5,451,453).

The common strand is that all these passages link the highest good to the idea of a world. It is happiness in accordance with the morality *of all* that is to be aimed at in willing the highest good. The highest good is to be realized then in a world, that is, in a social commonwealth, and not simply in a person.

Now, there is again the compatibility issue. Is it inconsistent or contradictory to treat the highest good as both an individual and a social end? Can this object of the will refer both to a goal for a person, for one will, and to a goal for the world, for the wills of all? Kant apparently did not find it contradictory to speak in the same sentence of the highest good for one person and the highest good for the world. What would be wrong is to deny either one of these interpretations of the highest good. To argue that the highest good is not an individual end does not do justice to the context in which the highest good is introduced in the second *Critique*. Happiness there is said to be a required part of the highest good not only "in the partial eyes of a person who makes himself his end but even in the judgment of an impartial reason, which impartially regards persons in the world as ends-in-themselves" (CPR,114/5,110). The happiness at stake in the highest good is both personal happiness and the happiness of others. The notion of the highest good as world must include a person's own happiness, his or her highest good. So perhaps the role of the highest good as social end encompasses and makes unnecessary any mention of the highest good as personal end. Yet, it seems helpful that both these roles be recognized. It is a person's own happiness, his or her own highest good, at stake in discussions of the object of the will. For instance, "the maxims of virtue and those of one's own happiness are wholly heterogeneous . . . even though they belong to a highest good" (CPR,117/5,112). It would be a mistake to fail to acknowledge that the highest good is posited as a personal end.

That said however, it is clearly the social role of the highest good that is most visible in Kant's writings. It is impossible to "argue away" this social role of the highest good in favor of some other role. There are at least the following three reasons for believing that the role of the highest good as world, as social end, takes precedence over its role as personal end. First, there is more textual evidence that the highest good is to be sought for all in the world than there is that it is to be sought for an individual person. Second, the notion of the highest good as social end is more compatible with its description as final end than is the notion of the highest good as individual end. The second task of the highest good is to serve as the final or ultimate end, and as final end, the highest good is the entirety of all ends. As such, it seems more likely to be a social goal than an individual goal. It makes more sense to consider the highest good as a final end if each person is pursuing a social goal, universal happiness in accordance with morality (that is, all ends). It is harder to comprehend how the highest good is a final end if each is pursuing a personal goal, his or her happiness in accordance with morality (that is, not all ends). Third, the role of the highest good as social end is truer to Kant's language in describing the highest good than is the notion of the highest good as individual end. Kant often uses the term *Weltbeste* to refer to the highest good.[24] *Weltbeste*, best world, can only be a synonym for the highest good if the highest good refers to a world, a social community. It is not a synonym for the highest good if the highest good refers only to a person's happiness in accordance with his or her worth. Hence, for these reasons, it is important to recognize that the highest good in its role as a social end takes priority over its role as an individual end.

III. Importance of the Highest Good

If the debate among the critics is treated in these general terms—Is the highest good important or unimportant to Kant's ethics?—then at least the following critics must be mentioned. Those arguing for the importance of the highest good include John Silber, Mary-Barbara Zeldin, Gerald Barnes, and R. Z. Friedman.[25] Those arguing for the unimportance of the highest good include L. W. Beck, Thomas Auxter, and Jeffrie Murphy.[26] However, the issue is not this simple and hence, this section looks at three ways in which the issue has been discussed. First, is the highest good the determining ground of the will? Related to this, does the highest good provide content for the will, or act as the material of the will? Second, does the highest good specify obligations or duties? Third, does the highest good have important practical consequences?

The first issue is whether the highest good acts as a determining ground of the will and/or as the content or material of the will. The concern is that if the highest good acts as the determining ground of the will and especially if it is also the material of the will, then the result will be heteronomy. If the autonomous will is one which is self-governing, which gives the law unto itself, which is not determined to action by its desire for any object, then it seems that a will cannot remain autonomous if the highest good is its determining ground and its material. The most serious threat seems to be in allowing the highest good to act as determining ground of the will. If the highest good determines the will to action then it does not really matter whether the highest good is the material content of the will or not (though if it is, the charge of heteronomy is perhaps more obvious). Whether it is the content of the will or not, insofar as the highest good determines the will, the result seems to be heteronomy. Something other than the will is determining the will to action. However, if the highest good is not the determining ground of the will then, as far as heteronomy is concerned, it does not seem to matter whether or not the highest good is the material of the will. Perhaps the highest good can act as the material content of the will without threatening the will's autonomy, as long as that content is not the determining ground of the will.[27] Yet, it is largely due to the charge of heteronomy that critics have examined these questions concerning the role of the highest good.

These two passages are the crucial ones:

> Consequently, though the highest good may be the entire *object* of a pure practical reason, i.e., of a pure will, it is still not to be taken as the *determining ground* of the pure will; the moral law alone must be seen as the ground for making the highest good and its realization or promotion the object of the pure will (CPR,113/5,109).

> But it is self-evident not merely that, if the moral law is included as the supreme condition in the concept of the highest good, the highest good is then the object, but also that the concept of it and the idea of its existence as possible through our practical reason are likewise the determining ground of the pure will. This is because the moral law, included and thought in this concept, and no other object, determines the will as required by the principle of autonomy (CPR,114/5,109-10).

The claims are these. The highest good is the object of the will. It is left unsaid whether this means that the highest good is the content or material of the will. In addition, the highest good *is not* the determining ground of the will; only the moral law itself is. Nevertheless, if the moral law is contained in the highest good then the highest good *is* the determining ground of the will. These claims make it necessary to recall parts of what has been discussed earlier, namely, what it means to be an object of the will and whether or not the moral law is contained in the highest good. Supposing that the moral law is so contained, these passages seem to be contradictory.

Apparently, they maintain both that the highest good is not the determining ground of the will and that it is the determining ground of the will.

First, section I showed that the highest good is defined as the end or object of the pure will. Chapter 3, section I, claimed that when the term "end" is defined, these terms are used interchangeably: object, end, material. To be an end is to be the material of the will and to be the material of the will is to be the object of the will (CPR,42,26/5,41,27). Therefore, the object of the will is the will's end, its material content.

Silber refers to the highest good as "the material object of volition."[28] Zeldin calls it "the object and end of an absolute, factually given command."[29] Even those who object to the identification of the highest good as content or material of the will do so for reasons that concern the possible consequences of such an identification and not because the identification itself seems wrong. It is what would follow from calling the highest good the content or material of the will that keeps some from recognizing it to be such. For instance, Murphy argues that the highest good cannot "function as a necessary content for the form of moral volition."[30] He seems thus to deny that the highest good is the content or object of the will. But in fact, the point of his claim is to deny that the highest good is the *necessary* object of the will although he admits that the highest good may be the object of the will.[31] Murphy insists that the highest good cannot be a necessary object because as such it would determine the will by nonformal content.[32] His real concern is that the highest good should not be the determining ground of the will. This means, in his terms, that the highest good can be the object or content of the will but not the necessary object or content of the will. Ultimately, Murphy is not objecting to the status of the highest good as object, content, or material of the will.

Beck and Friedman also seem to resist calling the highest good the content or material of the will. Both insist that the concept of the highest good is not an attempt on Kant's part to extend the realm of moral obligation by specifying a content or an object of the moral law.[33] But for both of them, the real danger lies not in identifying the highest good as the content of the will but in what seems to follow; namely, that as content of the will, the highest good determines the will or is necessary to the enumeration of moral duties. Beck says that the highest good "is necessary to the moral disposition, but not to the definition of duty."[34] Friedman says the highest good is necessary as the "condition of the possibility of the moral law."[35] Hence, again, the real concern of these critics is not to deny that the highest good is the material content of the will but to insist that the highest good does not act as the determining ground of the will.

The assumption seems to be that it is dangerous to label the highest good the content of the will because this is taken to mean the necessary content or the content determining the will to action. Chapter 3 showed that to be an end, an object, is to be a determining ground of the will. To generate a *moral* duty, a material object as a determining ground of the will must work in conjunction with or follow from the moral law. Hence, the idea of humanity is a determining ground of the will and generates moral duties, not by itself (that would be heteronomy) but in conjunction with, because it follows from, the form of the moral law. So it is the same presumably with the highest good as object or content of the will. As object of the will, the highest good is the will's material content. As such, it determines the will to action. Murphy, Beck, and Friedman are right to conclude that once the highest good is labelled the content of the will, it follows that the highest good functions as the determining ground of the will. The real question is, can the highest good be the determining ground of the will without resulting in heteronomy?

Second, it is clear that the moral law is contained in the highest good. It is because the moral law is said to be a part of the highest good that the charges of contradiction and heteronomy have arisen. The highest good includes virtue and happiness. Morality is the first condition of the highest good and happiness is the second element (CPR,123/5,119). The highest good is described as happiness in accordance with the purest morality (TP,46/8,279) and as happiness proportioned to obedience to duty (Rel.4/6,5). The long passage above from the second *Critique* says that the moral law is "included and thought in" the concept of the highest good (CPR,114/5,110). The parts of the highest good are "maxims of virtue and those of . . . happiness" (CPR,117/5,112). Thus, the first condition or part of the highest good is virtue or morality, in other words, actions or a life in accord with the moral law. The highest good contains the moral law in that one of its elements, virtue or morality, refers to a pure will acting for the sake of duty, for the sake of the moral law. There is no way to interpret the highest good as apart from, not involving, the moral law.

The question then is whether or not the texts are contradictory in saying both that the highest good is and is not a determining ground of the pure practical will. In fact, there is no contradiction or at least the apparent contradiction is not serious. By *itself*, as object of the will, the highest good is not the determining ground of the will. No object, not even the highest good, by itself can act to determine the will without resulting in heteronomy. However, *together with* the moral law, because it contains the moral law and is an object dictated by the moral law, the highest good is the determining ground of the will. There is no real contradiction here if it is recognized that the highest good is understood differently when it is said not to be a determining ground than it is when said to be a determining ground.

This is similar to the way in which the third and fourth antinomies of theoretical reason are resolved (A531-32/B559-60). In the first *Critique*, it is said that there is no real contradiction between the statements of the antinomies. Rather, the opposing statements in

Antinomies 3 and 4 are both true even though they seem to be contradictory. The statements of the antinomies can both be true because the object in question can be thought about in two ways. The search for the unconditioned can proceed towards a homogeneous condition within the realm of appearances or one can posit a heterogeneous, intelligible condition, not itself in the realm of appearances. So, to paraphrase Antinomy 3, it is true that there is natural causality (in the realm of appearances) but it is also true that there is freedom (regarded as an intelligible cause, outside the realm of appearances).

Here, concerning the claim that the highest good is and is not a determining ground of the will, the so-called contradiction is only an apparent one. Both sides, both opposing claims, are true when it is recognized that there are two ways of understanding the object in question. Granted, there is no mention here of homogeneous and heterogeneous conditions. Like the Antinomies however, there is a lack of clarity about where the object is to be found but no real contradiction between the statements about the object.

The highest good thought of simply as the object of the will cannot determine the will. No object, not even an object of moral value, can determine the will to action and have the result be a moral action. But, when it is recalled that the highest good is not simply an object, rather it is the object required by the moral law itself and it includes the moral law, then it can determine the will. In the first case, the highest good is taken to be an object desired by the will. In the second case, the highest good is an object required or posited as necessary by the will. It is not a random object in this sense and so, because the pure practical will dictates this object for itself, an object which cannot be realized apart from the pure practical will, this object can be called a determining ground of the will.[36] Therefore, the highest good, thought of as an object separate from the form of the moral law, cannot be a determining ground of the will.

But the highest good, thought of as an object required by the form of the moral law and realized only through the form of the moral law, can be a determining ground of the will.

The response to the charge of heteronomy is very nearly the same. In fact, there is no heteronomy involved in the claim that the highest good acts to determine the will. The reason is due to the peculiar nature of the highest good.

Heteronomy is present when something other than the will determines the will to action. This "something other" can be rational or empirical but in all cases, it is something separate from or apart from the will which determines the will (Gr.109/4,441-42; CPR,34,41/5,33,40). In short, when the will is not acting to determine itself to action, the result is heteronomy.

Now, the highest good as a determining ground of the will must be understood to be a something other if heteronomy is to be the result. However, the highest good is not a something other; it is not other than, apart from, separate from the pure will itself or the moral law. It is the moral law objectified, understood as a completed object. In any case, the highest good is dictated by the will. It is an object made necessary by the will and brought about only through the will. It is the content of the will as dictated by the form of the will, the moral law. Therefore, there is no heteronomy because there is nothing other than the will determining the will to action. The will acts autonomously when the highest good is its determining ground because the highest good is a required object of the moral law and because it is not separate from but contains the moral law. More simply, the highest good is not "other than" the will. It, like the moral law, is generated by, a product of, the will or pure practical reason. So when the highest good determines the will, it is the will determining itself to action. Hence, there is only "apparent" heteronomy here, like there was apparent contradiction earlier, until the real nature of the highest good is exposed.

The second issue involving the highest good concerns its role in specifying obligations or duties. The relationship between the highest good and duty is discussed in two ways. First, the question is whether or not it is a duty for finite rational beings to pursue the highest good. It is asked whether human beings are commanded, that is, whether it is a moral duty, to seek the highest good. Second, the question is whether or not the highest good helps define a person's duties. Here it is asked whether a duty to pursue the highest good posits new duties or more duties than are already commanded by the moral law. These questions involve clarifying whether human beings have a duty to pursue the highest good and whether, if a duty, the highest good would generate new or additional duties.

Lewis White Beck and Jeffrie Murphy are two critics who argue that there is no duty to pursue the highest good. Both Beck and Murphy acknowledge that their argument runs counter to Kant's explicit claims. Thus, the debate over whether or not it is a duty to pursue the highest good is not a debate within or among Kant's texts. It seems to be recognized by all that Kant claims there is a duty to pursue the highest good. Those who argue there is no such duty are arguing that Kant ought not to have recognized a duty to seek the highest good.

Beck's and Murphy's arguments are these. Beck claims that Kant was deceived into thinking human beings have a moral duty to promote the highest good distinct from those duties dictated by the form of the moral law alone.[37] Beck argues that there should be no separate command to seek the highest good apart from the command to act out of respect for the law.[38] His point is that whatever duties human beings have must be dictated by the form of the moral law. To say there is a duty to seek the highest good seems to define a duty in terms of the content of the law. Hence, Beck concludes that there cannot be a special duty to promote the highest good since all duties must follow from the form of the moral law. However, to counter Beck's claim, a critic could argue that the categorical imperative already defines a duty in terms of the object of the duty: "Act in such a way that you always treat humanity, whether in your own person or in the person of any other, never simply as a means, but always at the same time as an end" (Gr.96/4,429; CPR,90/5,87). Therefore, there seems to be no reason why there cannot be a distinct duty defined in terms of an object that does not violate the priority of the form of the moral law in dictating duties.

Murphy's argument is that "we cannot be obligated to promote the highest good because we are in no way *able* to promote the highest good."[39] Murphy's point is one concerning the practical or even the physical possibility of carrying out such a duty. To counter Murphy's claim, a critic could argue that Kant is insisting only on a duty to pursue, not to attain, the highest good. Also, there is Kant's claim that human beings do not have duties that they are not able to carry out. Questions about physical abilities and powers are not relevant to considerations of categorical commands (CPR,38/5,37). On the other hand, on page 89 of *Religion*, there is a passage which seems to agree with Murphy's claim since it states that human beings do not know if the achievement of the highest good lies within their power or not. This point is then used as a way of explaining that the duty to promote the highest good is a special sort of duty.

The texts certainly state that people have a duty to promote the highest good. In the second *Critique*, the highest good is often referred to as the necessary object of the will. It is the "a priori necessary object" (CPR,118/5,114) and the "absolutely necessary object" (CPR,139/5,134). Unquestionably, Kant's writings maintain that the moral law requires human beings to further the highest good. For instance: "It is a priori (morally) necessary to bring forth the highest good through the freedom of the will" (CPR,117/5,113); "we *should* seek to further the highest good" (CPR,129/5,125); and "The moral law commands us to make the highest possible good in a world the final object of all our conduct"

(CPR,134/5,129). There are also places where the term "duty" is used to describe a person's relationship to the pursuit of the highest good. The second *Critique* states that: "we can hope for the highest good (to strive for which is our *duty* under the moral law" (ibid.; my emphasis). *Religion* asserts: "The idea of the highest good, inseparably bound up with the purely moral disposition, cannot be realized by man himself . . . yet he discovers within himself the *duty* to work for this end" (Rel.130/6,139; my emphasis). Thus, the evidence shows that in Kant's ethics there is a duty to pursue the highest good.[40] People are commanded by the moral law, by pure practical reason, to promote the highest good. This claim is more defensible now since the objections of Beck and Murphy have been overcome.

The problem next is whether or not this duty to pursue the highest good generates new or additional duties. On the one hand, if the duty to pursue the highest good generates no new duties, then it is of little practical significance to ethics. In other words, if all of a person's duties follow from the moral law, then the discovery of a duty to seek the highest good adds nothing new to the enumeration of a person's duties. It commands no more than, nothing other than, what is already commanded by the moral law and so it does not play a role in defining duties.[41]

On the other hand, if the duty to pursue the highest good does generate new duties or serve to define duties, then it seems to undermine the priority of the moral law. If the duty to seek the highest good is crucial to ethics because it specifies a new duty, a duty that is not posited by the moral law, then the role of the moral law in defining duties seems to be usurped. It is no longer the only definer of duties. This threat to the role of the moral law makes it difficult perhaps to argue that the duty to further the highest good commands more than what is already commanded by the moral law. Nevertheless, it can be argued that the duty to pursue the highest good goes beyond what the moral law commands and hence, that it does dictate duties.[42]

The way to resolve this issue is to recognize that the duty to promote the highest good is a special sort of duty. Prima facie, it is not like other duties dictated by the moral law. Perhaps it is possible to distinguish between "more" and "different" in the summary of the two views above. To command something more than the moral law, the duty to pursue the highest good would have to add to, contribute something new or additional to, the roster of duties. Presumably, this something more is not already commanded by the moral law. To command something different than the moral law, the duty to further the highest good would not have to add something new to the roster of duties. The object of its command may be something already implicitly or explicitly commanded by the moral law. The something different may be a restatement or a reorganization or a clarification of something already commanded by the moral law. In this way, to command something different is not the same as commanding something more.

The claim to be made here, in advance of any evidence for it, is that the duty to seek the highest good certainly commands something different but probably does not command something more. It is a special duty, a different sort of duty, though it is not clear that it dictates something new, or extra, or additional.[43] So, it may be true to say that the duty to seek the highest good commands no more than the moral law although it surely commands in a different way than the moral law. In this sense then, the duty to further the highest good generates duties.

The duty to promote the highest good is special or different in two ways. In both cases, the duty to pursue the highest good is a different sort of duty because the highest good is a different sort of object. In the first case, the highest good is a special sort of object because it is the final end. When considering the duty to strive for the highest good, it is said that "this determination of the will is of a special sort, namely, determination by the idea of the entirety of all ends" (TP,46n/8,280). The concept of a final end "while not multiplying men's duties, yet provides them with a special point of focus for the unification of all ends" (Rel.5/6,5). In other words, because the highest good is the final end, the duty to seek the highest good is unlike any other duties dictated by the moral law. The final end, as shown earlier, is the entirety or sum total of all ends. It is the sufficient condition of all other ends (Rel.6n/6,6). Hence, the duty to seek it is a different duty because its end is the sum total of all moral ends but it is not an additional duty since it does not multiply a person's duties. It is not an extra duty; it is a collective duty. Thus, a good argument can be made that the special nature of the duty to further the highest good is due to the special nature of the highest good as end. The pure will's final end is not this or that object of the will but all objects of the will.[44] Since the highest good is an object like no other (it is highest object, final end; that is, it is the object of a moral life, not a moral action), so the duty to pursue it is a duty like no other. Thus, the duty to promote the highest good is a special or different sort of duty though it need not be seen as (and Kant says it is not) an additional or extra duty.

In the second case, the duty to pursue the highest good is a special duty due to the special nature of the highest good as a social object or end. A person's duty to further the highest good does not resemble other duties because the end in this case is a social end, a moral world. The uniqueness of this duty to pursue the highest good is evident in two places in *Religion*:

1. It is a duty of a peculiar kind [*eine Pflicht von besonderer Art*] (*officium sui generis*) to unite oneself with an ethical commonwealth . . . a special business [must] be made of their union with one another for the self-same end, and of the establishment of a COMMONWEALTH under moral laws (Rel.139/6,151).

2. Now here we have a duty which is *sui generis* [*eine Pflicht von ihrer eignen Art*], not of men toward men,

> but of the human race toward itself. For the species of rational beings is objectively, in the idea of reason, destined for a social goal, namely, the production of the highest as a social good. But because the highest moral good cannot be achieved merely by the exertions of the single individual toward his own moral perfection, but requires rather a union of such individuals into a whole toward the same goal . . . the idea of such a whole, as a universal republic based on laws of virtue, is an idea completely distinguished from all moral laws . . . Hence this duty is distinguished from all others both in kind and in principle (Rel.89/6,97-98).

These passages make several claims, not all of which seem to be compatible, but consider the main point first. Fundamentally, these passages describe a way in which the duty to further the highest good is unique or special. It is a special duty, a duty *sui generis*, because the end of this duty is a social goal, a moral commonwealth. Again, it is said to be due to the special nature of the highest good as object that the duty to pursue the highest good is a special duty.

Looking beyond this point, it appears as if the uniqueness of the duty to pursue the highest good, treated as a social end, is understood in two ways. First, uniting oneself with an ethical commonwealth, that is, with others in an ethical commonwealth, is a special task. Presumably, the furthering of a person's other moral duties does not require joining together with others in creating a moral world. The second passage states that the highest good cannot be achieved by a single individual. No doubt, this duty to promote the highest good makes it necessary to work with others towards the achievement of the highest good.

Second, in describing the uniqueness of this duty *sui generis*, it is called a duty "not of men toward men, but of the human race toward itself." This suggests a different point about how the social nature of the highest good makes the duty to pursue the highest good a special duty. Here it is said that the duty to promote the highest good is a duty of the race, of mankind, and not of individuals.[45] Perhaps the social nature of the end makes the duty itself a social, collective, or group duty. It is however unclear how seriously this suggestion from passage two ought to be taken. While it is certainly a radical way of distinguishing the duty to further the highest good from all other duties, it is not clear that this passage represents Kant's overall view. Both of the two passages from *Religion* speak of "uniting oneself" and of "a union of such individuals into a whole." It is hard to see how the duty to pursue such a union of oneself with others arises if it is only a collective duty to further the highest good. There are too many passages in which the duty to pursue the highest good is considered to be the duty of each person to conclude that it is only a duty of the race.

One other point must be considered to complete the assessment of the role of the highest good in specifying duties. The argument so far is that the highest good is not something other than the moral law nor is the duty to seek it something more than the moral law commands, although it is something different than the moral law commands. To the charge of heteronomy, the response was that the highest good is not a thing separate from, apart, or other than the moral law. It is an object required by, posited by, the moral law. To the charge that the highest good usurps the role of the moral law as dictator of duties, the response was that the highest good does not generate new, additional, or extra duties. It does not create new duties which would otherwise not follow from the moral law. To the charge that the highest good is thus not necessary to ethics, the response was that the duty to pursue it is something special, something different, than the moral law commands and as such, it is necessary. The highest good is a final end, and a social end, and that distinguishes it from all other ends posited by the moral law and makes the duty to pursue it, a duty unlike all other duties specified by the moral law. Because the highest good is a unique end, the duty to pursue it is special, different.

It might be claimed that there is a contradiction in this reasoning. Perhaps it is contradictory to say that a thing which is not other than another thing is however different than that other thing. This reasoning is trying to "have it both ways" by denying that the highest good is separate from the moral law while at the same time affirming that the highest good is unique. However, the attempt to have it both ways is, it seems, a true reflection of Kant's ethics. Kant's writings maintain that the highest good is and is not the determining ground of the will. Kant's writings argue that the highest good is not foreign to, separate from, or other than the moral law though it is not the same as the moral law. It is the object of the moral law, the necessary, final object, though not the law itself. Kant's texts insist that the duty to seek this highest good is not more than or other than what the moral law requires although it is different than what the moral law dictates. It is special, it is *sui generis*. While this account is difficult and complex, it does not seem to be contradictory. There is no contradiction if something which is not separate from a thing is yet different from the thing and such is the case with the highest good and the moral law.

The third issue debated by many critics concerns whether or not the highest good has important practical consequences. Some ask whether the highest good is a necessary component of Kant's ethics[46] and others ask whether it is a useful notion in his ethics. Beck and Silber are perhaps the two best representatives of the extreme views on this issue. Beck insists that the highest good is not a practical concept and that it has no practical consequences in Kant's philosophy.[47] Silber argues that the concept of the highest good is important for ethical practice and that it is of central importance to Kant's ethics.[48]

There are many ways to address this question. This chapter has claimed that the highest good is assigned several roles in Kant's ethics and that the relationship between the highest good and duty or the moral law is at best a complex one. The conclusions reached here about the relative importance of the highest good are the result of these earlier discussions. One place to begin is to observe that Beck and Silber both seem to be assessing the importance of the highest good in terms of the effect it has on the practice of morality. Beck says the highest good contributes nothing to a person's deliberations about how to act and Silber claims that the highest good contributes to the practice of morality. It appears that both are evaluating the importance of the highest good in terms of a single task, that is, as if Kant's practical philosophy were concerned solely with the making of moral judgments.

But this implicit assumption can be denied. Quite apart from whether the highest good is important or unimportant to the process of moral judging, it may be that there are other tasks the highest good serves in practical philosophy. For instance, the highest good could still be of practical importance as object, and especially, as final object, of the will. Every act of the will has an object (CPR,34/5,34) and it is certainly of practical significance to name, define, and describe this object of the pure will. In particular, since reason is never satisfied with any conditioned object (CPR,112/5,108), it is important for practical reason to have an unconditioned object toward which it aims in its drive to completeness.[49]

Thus, whether or not the highest good is necessary to the exercise of moral judgment, of volition, there is still a good case to make that it is necessary to practical reason, and to the completion of a truly moral life. The highest good may contribute to a person's understanding of the ultimate goal of all moral actions. The success or failure of the highest good to directly determine the will is not sufficient proof of the importance or unimportance of the highest good.

But, in fact, the argument here must be even stronger. This chapter claimed that while the highest good is not *the* determining ground of the will or by *itself* the sole determining ground of the will, it works together with the moral law to determine the will. Ends are determining grounds of the will. Therefore, the highest good, as end, does play a role in determining the will. There may be moral judgments which do not involve the highest good (for example, should I keep this promise to X or not?). However, there is nothing about the nature or task of the highest good which makes it inappropriate to all moral judging. Thus, certainly, if in a person's willing, that person is concerned with the final end of all his or her willing or of a world in which there is only pure willing, then the highest good is a legitimate determining ground of the will, in conjunction with the moral law.

Based on these discussions of the nature and roles of the highest good and of the relationship between the highest good and the moral law, it follows that the highest good is of practical importance, to practical reason and to the will, especially in its role as object or end of the will. It is of practical importance in defining the final goal of the will, of morality, and of helping human beings to recognize the communal nature of that goal. If there is no action without an end and pure practical reason is distinguished by its pursuit of an unconditioned end, then the highest good is the highest, most important end of ethics. Since ends also act as determining grounds of the will, the highest good as an end dictated by the moral law (a moral end) acts in turn with the law to determine the will. Hence, the highest good as object, as end, as determining ground, is of practical importance to Kant's ethics.

Chapter Six

Problems with the Highest Good and Consequences of the Highest Good for Happiness

The discussion of the meaning and role of the highest good is complicated in part by the inexactness of Kant's language. There are at least three names for the highest good which seem to be used interchangeably: *summum bonum*, *höchste Gut*, and *Weltbeste*. It is easiest to see that the first two of these are identical. They are simply the Latin and the German terms meaning "highest good." The third term seems to translate into English as "best world" which may or may not be the same thing as the highest good but is not so self-evidently. Section I considers some of the difficulties involved in the names for the highest good and shows that these three terms are used to mean the same thing, that is, happiness in proportion to worth. Also, the English term "supreme good" is often substituted for *summum bonum* and for *höchste Gut* though Kant's texts offer a clear distinction between the supreme good [*das oberste Gut*] and the perfect or highest good [*das höchste Gut . . . bedeutet . . . das vollendete Gute*]. Hence, the appearance of the term "supreme good" in the English texts is considered in order to show that it ought not to be used as a substitute for *summum bonum*, namely, the highest good. Section II focuses on the description of the highest good as both "in" the world and "outside" the world. There is inexactness in the texts concerning the location of the highest good since it is posited to be in the world and in the intelligible world or in a future world. Section III shows how the discussion of the highest good illuminates the role of happiness in Kant's ethics.

I. Meaning of the Highest Good

The term used most frequently for the highest good is *höchste Gut.* For instance, the first *Critique* speaks of happiness in exact proportion to worth and calls it "the highest good [*das höchste Gut*]" (A814/B842).[1] It refers also to the "two elements of the highest derivative good [*beiden Elemente des höchsten abgeleiteten Guts*]" (A811/B839). Similarly, *Theory and Practice* calls the union of morality and happiness "the highest good possible in the world [*das höchste in der Welt mögliche Gut*]" (TP,46/8,279). The *Religion* directs persons to make "the highest good possible in the world [*das höchste in der Welt mögliche Gut*] your own final end" (Rel.7n/6,7). Thus, in these texts there is no confusion in the identification of the highest good since the term *höchste Gut* is used consistently. The questions that arise concerning the names for the highest good involve passages from the *Lectures*, and the second and third *Critiques*.

Consider the second *Critique* first. By and large, the description of the highest good raises no difficulties here. To the best of my knowledge, in all the passages except one, the only name used for the highest good is "*das höchste Gut.*"[2] The single exception is a passage which says in part: "a highest derived good (the best world) [*des höchsten abgeleiteten Guts (der besten Welt)*]" (CPR,130/5,125). In this passage, the highest good (*höchste Gut*) is identified with "*der besten Welt.*" The equating of the highest good with a kind of world raises two issues, one of terminology and one of meaning.

First, there is a point about terminology. *Der besten Welt* is apparently taken to be another name for *das höchste Gut.* The highest good is equivalent to a kind of world, the best world. There are other passages which identify the highest good with a kind of world though the exact words, *der besten Welt,* are not used again. As is shown in what follows, the highest good is called "the most perfect world [*die vollkommenste Welt*]" (LE,6/M,7) and "the best world [*Weltbeste*]" (CJ,304/5,453). These terms all make the same claim. All identify the highest good with the best, the most perfect, world. Thus, when this section claims that the highest good is called by the names *höchste Gut, summum bonum,* and *Weltbeste,* these other names for the best world (*der besten Welt, die vollkommenste Welt*) are included in *Weltbeste.*

Second, there is a point about meaning. The highest good is called the best world. We might ask whether or not this is legitimate although a reason is given for believing they mean the same thing.

The reason is this. Chapter 5 showed that the highest good serves in these two roles, among others: individual end and social end. The highest good is both personal happiness awarded in proportion to personal worth, and a world in which the happiness of all is awarded according to worth. The term *Weltbeste* emphasizes the fact that the highest good is a social end.

A passage from the second *Critique* (considered above) makes the point most succinctly. Kant distinguishes between the highest good for one person [*des höchsten Guts in einer Person*] and the highest good of a world [*das höchste Gut einer möglichen Welt*] (CPR,115/5,110). Given that the highest good plays the role of both an individual end and a social end, it is not surprising that at times the highest good is called "the best world." That is merely a way of recognizing the social nature of this goal of the highest good. The term *höchste Gut* is nonspecific with regard to whether it is an individual or a social goal, but "*Weltbeste*" makes specific the social, global nature of this goal.

In the *Lectures on Ethics*, the terms *summum bonum* and *höchste Gut* are used to refer to the highest good, happiness in proportion to worth. It is claimed that the moral systems of the ancients are based on the question: What constitutes the *summum bonum*? This *summum bonum* is only an Ideal, that is, the pattern, the idea, the archetype for all our concepts of the good (LE,6/M,7).[3] Then it is asked: What constitutes the highest good [*das höchste Gut*]? The answer is:

> The highest created good is the most perfect world [*Die vollkommenste Welt ist das höchste erschaffene Gut*] (ibid.).[4]
>
> In man therefore we must look for both happiness [*Glückseligkeit*] and worth [*Würdigkeit*], and when these are combined together, they are the highest good [*und wenn dieses zusammengenommen wird, so ist es das höchste Gut*] (ibid.).

In these passages, the terms *summum bonum* and *höchste Gut* are connected and both refer to the highest good, that is, the bringing together of happiness and worth. In addition, the most perfect world [*die vollkommenste Welt*], here identified with the highest created good, is no doubt a variation of the best world [*Weltbeste*]. This passage makes manifest the role of the highest good as a social end, a world to be brought about.

The third *Critique* speaks of the *höchste Gut* and *Weltbeste* and even of the *höchste Weltbeste*. In the references to the highest good, there is nothing that causes serious confusion to the understanding of the meaning or tasks of the highest good. There are several small points in the description of the highest good that deserve special mention but, most importantly, there is consistency here in the use of *höchste Gut* and *Weltbeste* to mean highest good.

These four claims are made:

1. The highest physical good possible in the world, to be furthered as a final purpose as far as in us lies, is

happiness, under the objective condition of the harmony of man with the law of *morality* as worthiness to be happy (CJ,301/5,450).[5]

2. a happiness of rational beings in harmony with the pursuit of moral laws, regarded as the highest good (CJ,302/5,451).[6]
3. We are *a priori* determined by reason to promote with all our powers the *summum bonum* (*Weltbeste*) (CJ,304/5,453).[7]
4. Of this kind is the *highest good* in the world, to be brought about by freedom (CJ,321/5,469).[8]

Three points to note are these. First, the first passage from above speaks of the highest *physical* good. As noted above, happiness in conformity with virtue is occasionally distinguished from a highest *original* good (CPR,130/5,125).[9] Happiness in conformity with virtue is the highest physical good or created good (LE,6/M,7) or derived good (CPR,130,133/5,125,128). Second, it is curious that the second passage from above refers to "*den höchsten Weltbesten*" which is translated in the English as "the highest good." This seems to be just a variation on *höchste Gut* and *Weltbesten* and so it seems safe to assume it is equivalent to the latter two. Finally, it should be noted in passage three from above that the English translation has added the words *summum bonum*, presumably to aid in the identification of the term, *Weltbeste*. While the text does not include these words, since the terms *summum bonum*, *höchste Gut*, and *Weltbeste* are used interchangeably, the insertion of *summum bonum* into the English translation is not a misrepresentation.

A second problem for the English reader is the tendency of translators to substitute for *summum bonum* and *höchste Gut* the term supreme good. This is in spite of the fact that, in the second *Critique*, it is said that while the term "*höchste*" is ambiguous, Kant understands by *höchste Gut*, the complete good and not the supreme good (CPR,114-15/5,110-11). Thus, as the following discussion will show, at those places where *summum bonum* and *höchste Gut* are identified as the supreme good, it is the translators (not Kant) who are making this erroneous identification. In fact, Kant does not, and we should not, confuse the highest good with the supreme good.

In the *Lectures on Ethics*, the term supreme good is introduced in the English translation but not found in the German. For example, when it is claimed that the ground of the moral systems of the ancients lies in "*die Frage vom summo bono*"; the English says, "the question of . . . the *summum bonum*-the Supreme Good" (LE,6/M,7). When it is asked: "*Worin besteht das höchste Gut?*"; the English reads, "What constitutes the Supreme Good?" Similarly, the text considers "*das höchste erschaffene Gut*" and the English translation reads "the supreme created good" (ibid.); the text specifies the two elements of the "*höchsten Gutes*" and the translation reads the Supreme Good (LE,8/M,10). In short, the English translation of the *Lectures* substitutes supreme good for *summum bonum* and for *höchste Gut*. There is no apparent reason for this substitution and the result of such a substitution is that the English reader familiar with the *Lectures* and the second *Critique* is confused about the relationship between the supreme good and the highest good.

There is further evidence that English translators sometimes translate *höchste Gut* as supreme good in Kemp Smith's translation of the first *Critique*.[10] In the Canon section of the *Critique*, Kemp Smith translates "*des höchsten ursprünglichen Guts*" as "the supreme *original* good"; "*des höchsten abgeleiteten Guts*" as "the supreme derivative good"; and "*das höchste Gut*" as "the supreme good" (A810/B838; A811/B839; A814/B842). Again, this labeling of the highest good as the supreme good does not contribute to our overall understanding of Kant's doctrine of the highest good. There is no reason to think that Kant identified the *summum bonum* or *höchste*

Gut with the supreme good [*oberste Gut*]. Even in his earlier works, Kant consistently uses the terms *höchste Gut*, *summum bonum*, and *Weltbeste* to refer to the highest good, yet not the term *oberste Gut*. It is the fault of the English translations if there is uncertainty as to whether or not the highest good is the supreme good.

II. Location of the Highest Good

By far the most serious problem in defining the highest good concerns the location of the highest good. The highest good is spoken of "in the world" and "in a future world" or "in the intelligible world." The question can rightly be asked whether the highest good is an end realizable in this world (a sensible world) or in another world (an intelligible world). Several critics have recognized that the texts speak of the highest good in the world and of the highest good out of the world.[11] Some of them have used these two ways of speaking as evidence of two meanings of the highest good.[12] Certainly, there is ambiguity concerning the location of the highest good. However, this ambiguity does not compromise either the definition of the highest good as happiness in conformity with virtue or the four tasks of the highest good discussed in Chapter 5. This ambiguity does compromise the understanding of *where* the highest good is to be realized and perhaps also the understanding of *when* it might be achieved.

Sometimes, the highest good is spoken of only as in the world (*Theory and Practice*). Other times, it is spoken of only as in a future world or in an intelligible world (*Critique of Pure Reason*). Yet, perhaps the best indications of inexactness on this issue are those works which characterize the highest good as both in the world and in a future world (*Critique of Practical Reason*, *Religion Within the Limits of Reason Alone*). Let me document this problem involving the location of the highest good.

Because the highest good has been called the final end of the pure will and the object of the moral law, it might be taken for granted that the highest good is a realizable object in the world. That is, it seems to follow that the highest good is something people can work to achieve and that it is achievable in the sensible realm in which morality and happiness are acted out. Indeed, the highest good is frequently referred to in this way. The *Critique of Practical Reason* speaks of the "achievement of the highest good in the world" (CPR,126/5,122). It claims that "the highest good is possible in the world" (CPR,129/5,125) and that the practical law "requires the existence of the highest good possible in the world" (CPR,139/5,134). It also refers to "the endeavor to produce and to further the highest good in the world" (CPR,130/5,126).

These claims are repeated in *Theory and Practice* and *Religion. Theory and Practice* refers to "the highest good possible in the world" (TP,46/8,279). *Religion* speaks of "the idea of a highest good in the world" (Rel.4/6,5) and of "the highest good possible in the world" (Rel.6n,7n/6,7n) and of the "highest good possible on earth" (Rel.126/6,136). Thus, in these passages, human beings have reason to work toward the achievement of the highest good possible in the natural world. The goal, the final end, is to be realized in this world, in the sensible world, and does not require the positing of a future world or an intelligible world.

However, there are other passages which state just as emphatically that the highest good is possible only in a future world or an intelligible world. For instance, the first *Critique* says that happiness distributed in exact proportion to worth is "possible only in the intelligible world" (A811/B839). It is to be understood "as a future world" (ibid.) and as "an intelligible world only" (A814/B842). The second *Critique* makes similar claims. It maintains that human beings are obliged "to seek at such distance—namely, in the context of an intelligible world—the possibility of the highest good" (CPR,119/5,115). It notes, by way of explanation, that happiness "cannot (as far as our own capacity is concerned) be reached in this life" (CPR,133/5,129) and that the well-being proportionate to morality "is thought of as attainable only in eternity" (ibid.). It claims that the possibility of a connection between morality and the expectation of proportionate happiness "belongs wholly to the supersensuous relations of things" (CPR,124/5,119). Finally, *Religion* states that:

> As regards men's very natural expectation of an allotment of happiness proportional to a man's moral conduct, especially in view of the many sacrifices of the former which must be undergone for the sake of the latter, he [God] promises a reward for these sacrifices in a future world (Rel.149/6,161).

Here the claim is that the highest good or happiness in proportion to worth is to be realized only in an intelligible world, a future world, or in eternity. The reason for removing the highest good from this sensible world has to do with one of its components, happiness. The natural world most likely cannot be brought into harmony with morality in this world. Happiness most likely will not be awarded in proportion to morality in this world. Hence, the achievement of happiness in proportion to worth and so the highest good itself is said to take place outside of this world, in an intelligible world. In fact, theoretical reason "finds it impossible to conceive" of a perfect connection between morality and happiness in the natural world (CPR,150/5,145). But theoretical reason "cannot objectively decide" whether this connection is possible in the natural world or whether the connection requires the assumption of a wise Author of nature (CPR,151/5,145). Hence, a subjective condition of reason becomes involved, an interest of practical reason, and so human beings voluntarily decide to posit God's existence. The point seems to be that it is not impossible for the highest good to be in the world but it is easier to conceive of it outside the world and so doing also satisfies an interest of practical reason.

The highest good is identified in one other way which bears on the question of its location. This new identification does not resolve the ambiguity concerning where the highest good is to be realized though it favors one location over the other. The new identification is this. The highest good is equated with the Kingdom of God. This identification occurs both in the second *Critique* and in *Religion*. The second *Critique* says that Christianity gives "a concept of the highest good (the Kingdom of God)" (CPR,133/5,127-28). Later it speaks of our desire "to promote the highest good (to bring the Kingdom of God to us)" (CPR,135/5,130). The *Religion*, in a passage concerned with the realizing of a world in which happiness is awarded in proportion to worth, refers to this world as: "such a commonwealth, being a KINGDOM OF GOD" (Rel.139/6,151).

The identification of the highest good with the Kingdom of God lends support to the view that the highest good is outside the world. When Christianity is discussed, the texts sometimes equate the highest good with the Kingdom of God. The Kingdom of God is outside this world. For instance, the second *Critique* contains this phrase: "an intelligible world (the Kingdom of God)" (CPR,142/5,137). The *Religion* speaks of "the visible representation (the schema) of an invisible kingdom of God on earth" (Rel.122/6,131). This passage seems to refer to a visible representation on earth of what is an invisible Kingdom of God. In what follows this passage, it is said that the Teacher of the Gospel reveals only the moral aspect of "the kingdom of God on earth" while the other part of what persons wish for, namely, happiness, is not to be realized on earth (Rel.125/6,134). Although the phrase "the kingdom of God on earth" is used, it does not seem to follow that the Kingdom of God is to be realized in the world or on earth. The text mentions a *representation* on earth of the Kingdom of God and refers to a *part* of the Kingdom of God that may be realizable or acted out on earth (namely, the moral aspect). But both of these claims still imply that the Kingdom of God itself and *in toto* is not located on earth or in the world. Rather the Kingdom of God is an intelligible world, it is a future world, it is the "kingdom of heaven" (Rel.124/6,134). If the Kingdom of God is an intelligible world, not located on earth or in the world, then the highest good insofar as it has been equated with the Kingdom of God is itself in an intelligible world, not located on earth or in the world. Thus, the identification of the highest good with the Kingdom of God tends to emphasize the claim that the highest good is possible only in an intelligible world though it by no means obviates the claims concerning the highest good in the world.

This problem concerning the location of the highest good cannot be resolved. This much is clear. The highest good is spoken of as if it is in the world and as if it is outside the world. However, the fault for this ambiguity seems to lie with reason, not Kant. It is not that Kant could not make up his mind whether the highest good is possible in the world or outside the world. It is rather reason which is unable to determine whether the highest good is possible in the world or only outside the world. The problem is that we cannot know that the unity posited by the highest good is impossible in the natural world. It is at least possible that the highest good might be realized in the world although it is easier to conceive of its realization outside the world. In sum, there are three reasons for preferring an account which places the highest good outside the world. First, such an account is more "conceivable" to theoretical reason. Second, such an account satisfies an interest of practical reason. Third, such an account makes sense of the identification of the highest good with the Kingdom of God. Thus, while the texts (and reason) allow that the highest good may be possible in the world, there is evidence to suggest that the texts (and reason) generally think of it outside the world.

III. Consequences for Happiness

The highest good is an important part of Kant's practical philosophy although his discussion of it is sometimes vague and inconsistent. The highest good is especially important for my purposes because it is tied to the issue of happiness. There are two ways in which the discussion of the highest good sheds light on Kant's treatment of happiness in ethics.

First, the highest good includes happiness as one of its elements. The highest good is a moral end, the final end, of the will. As an end, the highest good serves also as a determining ground of the will. The highest good is good and its pursuit is a duty, perhaps the highest duty or at least the most all-encompassing duty. Since happiness is contained in the highest good, happiness as part of this larger whole is good and its pursuit is the object of a duty. It is a direct duty, a moral duty, to will to further the highest good and in so doing a person is willing to further happiness in proportion to virtue. This amounts to the strongest evidence there is that happiness is part of a moral end and a legitimate object of a direct moral duty. Of course, it is not happiness alone that is treated so positively but happiness conditioned by worthiness. Nevertheless, happiness is a constituent part of the highest end. That gives happiness, as conditioned, as part of the whole which is the highest good, an important role in ethics.

I have claimed that in Kant's texts there are four roles for happiness in ethics. Happiness can be treated in its role as: a principle of ethics, a natural end, a means to a moral end, and a part of a moral end. This last task for happiness is obviously its most important task. While happiness is acknowledged to be valuable as a natural end, and even as indirectly the object of a duty (as means to a moral end), it is only in its last role that happiness is seen to be valuable in ethics for what it is in itself. That is, it is found to be directly valuable as part of a moral end. In Kant's treatment of the highest good, happiness is shown to have a positive role to play. In light of his discussion of the highest good, it would be impossible, that is, wrong, to argue that happiness is nothing or that happiness plays no positive role in Kant's ethics. Happiness plays several positive roles in Kant's ethics, and of particular importance is its role as part of the highest moral end.

Second, the account of the highest good suffers from unclarity surrounding where the highest good is to be realized. The highest good is spoken of both in the world (in the sensible world) and outside the world (in an intelligible world). This same unclarity was noted in the account of the meaning of happiness. Sometimes happiness is spoken of in terms of inclination and pleasure (sensible states) and sometimes it is spoken of in terms of moral happiness, self-contentment, and bliss (intelligible or moral states). Sometimes happiness is said to be realized in the sensible world and other times it is claimed happiness cannot be realized on earth (Rel.125/6,134).

There is certainly some connection between these issues. The lack of clarity regarding the meaning of happiness possibly contributed to the ambiguity concerning where the highest good may be realized. Or it may be that the connection is the reverse. Perhaps the inexactness concerning the location of the hoped-for highest good led to uncertainty regarding the definition of happiness.

Let me consider how these ambiguities might be related. One possibility is that the ambiguity in the meaning of happiness came first. As evidence for this, it might be noted that the ambiguity in the definition of happiness occurs earlier in Kant's works than does evidence of the ambiguity in the highest good. In one of Kant's ethical fragments written between 1775 and 1781 happiness is understood to be an intelligible state. Yet, in the same time period, happiness is described as "the physical good" (LE,8/M,10). On the other hand, the ambiguity involving the location of the highest good is not obvious in Kant's writings until 1788. The first *Critique* speaks of the highest good in an intelligible world and it is not until the second *Critique* (and *Religion*, and *Theory and Practice*) that the highest good is also spoken about as possible in the world.

Also, there is a certain logical connection between these two ambiguities if the ambiguity in the definition of happiness came first. If the ambiguity in the meaning of happiness came first then the whole in which happiness is a part might also be expected to suffer from ambiguity. An ambiguity in the definition of happiness might have logically carried over to the highest good in which it is a part.

On the other hand, a second possibility is that the ambiguity in the highest good came first. Many have seen Kant's concept of the highest good as an attempt to bring together the natural and the moral sides of the human being.[13] In this notion, it is said, human beings overcome the dichotomy of their phenomenal/sensible and noumenal/moral sides. The notion of the highest good is not a necessary one for pure wills or holy wills but is a necessary one for human wills. Thus, in the highest good, happiness has a sensible meaning. If the possibility of the highest good is then postponed to an intelligible world, the meaning of happiness becomes ambiguous. Happiness can hardly be a natural, sensible state in an intelligible or future world. In this way, it may be that Kant was led to think of different senses of happiness due to reason's inability to determine where the highest good is to be realized.

It is worth recalling Kant's reasons for postponing the highest good to an intelligible or future world. It is claimed that theoretical reason cannot decide if the highest good is possible in the natural world or only in an intelligible world on the assumption of a wise Author of nature. Then two reasons are offered for favoring the latter explanation. First, the happiness component of the highest good cannot be reached in this life (CPR,133/5,129). It is thought of as attainable only in eternity. The explanation is that happiness cannot be realized on earth because human nature is never content (CJ,279-80/5,430). Second, an interest of practical reason becomes involved. The interest of practical reason lies in determining the will with respect to the final and perfect end (CPR,124/5,120). To ensure the possibility of the highest good, it must be shown that there is a necessary connection between virtue and happiness. In the sensible world there can be at best only a contingent connection and so to satisfy the interest of practical reason (which has primacy over the interest of theoretical reason)[14] the highest good must be posited in an intelligible world. Practical reason's interest tips the balance in favor of a highest good outside the natural world.

I have not attempted to reach any conclusion as to which possible account of the connection between happiness and the highest good is more compelling. What I have argued for is that there is certainly a connection between these two issues. It is curious that the primary meaning of happiness is that of a sensible well-being while the preferred location of the highest good, in which happiness is a component, is in an intelligible world. It is not by accident that there is an ambiguity in the definition of happiness *and* an ambiguity in the location of the highest good.

Notes

Introduction

1. John R. Silber, "The Ethical Significance of Kant's *Religion*," part of the introduction to Greene and Hudson translation of Kant's *Religion Within the Limits of Reason Alone* (New York: Harper, 1960), cxii-cxiii, n85.

2. Silber, "The Ethical Significance of Kant's *Religion*," cxiii, n85.

3. Lewis White Beck, *A Commentary on Kant's Critique of Practical Reason* (Chicago: University of Chicago Press, 1960), 231.

4. H. J. Paton, *The Categorical Imperative* (Chicago: University of Chicago Press, 1948), 48.

5. H. H. Schroeder, "Some Common Misinterpretations of the Kantian Ethics," *The Philosophical Review* 49 (1940), 424-46.

6. Schroeder, "Some Common Misinterpretations of the Kantian Ethics," 424-25.

7. Theodore M. Greene, "The Historical Context and Religious Significance of Kant's *Religion*," part of the introduction to Greene and Hudson translation of Kant's *Religion Within the Limits of Reason Alone* (New York: Harper, 1960), lxiii.

8. Viggo Rossvaer, *Kant's Moral Philosophy* (Oslo: Universitetsforlaget, 1979), 110. However, Rossvaer offers no footnote or bibliographical reference to support his accusation.

9. Woodbridge Riley, *Men and Morals: The Story of Ethics* (New York: F. Ungar Publ. Co., 1960), 304.

10. Riley, *Men and Morals*, 300.

11. Thomas Higgins, S. J., *Basic Ethics* (Milwaukee: Bruce Publishing Company, 1968), 111.

12. William A. Banner, *Ethics: An Introduction to Moral Philosophy* (New York: Charles Scribner's Sons, 1968), 100.

13. Thomas Auxter, *Kant's Moral Teleology* (Macon: Mercer University Press, 1982), 82.

14. Auxter, *Kant's Moral Teleology*, 9.

15. See Auxter, *Kant's Moral Teleology*, 10, where he says the highest good is "the least suitable and most dispensable concept in Kant's moral theory."

16. Keith Ward, *The Development of Kant's View of Ethics* (Oxford: B. Blackwell, 1972), 1.

17. Ward, *The Development of Kant's View of Ethics*, 95.

18. Marcus G. Singer, *Generalization in Ethics* (London: Eyre & Spottiswoode Ltd., 1963), 251-52.

19. Singer, *Generalization in Ethics*, 263.

20. Bruce Aune, *Kant's Theory of Morals* (Princeton: Princeton University Press, 1979), 120.

21. Rossvaer, *Kant's Moral Philosophy*, 129.

22. Silber, "The Ethical Significance of Kant's *Religion*," cxiii, n85.

23. John R. Silber, "The Importance of the Highest Good in Kant's Ethics," *Ethics* 73 (1963), 195.

24. Silber, "The Importance of the Highest Good in Kant's Ethics," 195.

25. John E. Atwell, *Ends and Principles in Kant's Moral Thought* (Dordrecht: Nijhoff, 1986), xii.

26. Atwell, *Ends and Principles in Kant's Moral Thought*, 1.

Chapter 1

1. Norbert Fischer, in "Tugend und Glückseligkeit: Zu ihrem Verhältnis bei Aristoteles und Kant," *Kant-Studien* 74

(1983) considers several meanings of happiness for Kant; among them, happiness as the highest good (3,9) and intellectual happiness (10).

2. Donald Walhout, in "Kant's Conception of Nonmoral Good," *Southwestern Journal of Philosophy* 3 (1972), 12, considers that Kant speaks of happiness hedonistically but concludes that this cannot be the real meaning he assigns happiness since happiness covers all good except virtue. It will be shown that Kant has a sensible, hedonistic account of happiness and an intelligible, nonhedonistic account of happiness though I conclude from the texts that Kant is apparently more satisfied with (finds less reason to qualify) the former than the latter.

3. Viggo Rossvaer, *Kant's Moral Philosophy* (Oslo: Universitetsforlaget, 1979), notes these two ways of considering happiness. He refers to happiness viewed as "sensuous satisfaction" and viewed as "an unrealizable ideal, i.e. actually as bliss" (134). However, on the same page, Rossvaer speaks of the "dual nature of Kant's concept of happiness" and means by it something else. There he refers to happiness regarded first as unceasing pleasure and second as an organized whole providing the greatest possible satisfaction. I take the first distinction—that between sensible and intelligible happiness—to be more fundamental.

4. See also Rel.69n/6,75n.

5. See, for instance, the *Lectures on Ethics*, where Kant says that good and ill-fortune depend on ourselves and on the attitude we adopt towards them (LE,145/M,182). We cannot claim greater happiness in this life, he says, than by maintaining a cheerful frame of mind in whatever ill befalls us. Note here that Kant's term is *Glück*, not *Glückseligkeit*.

6. Gary Watson, "Kant on Happiness in the Moral Life," *Philosophy Research Archives* 9 (1983), 81, says that happiness is "one's basic *attitude* toward one's life on the whole." Watson concludes that happiness understood as contentment refers to a psychological state and can be distinguished from a notion of happiness that refers to the satisfaction of inclinations. However, in the passages which speak of happiness as contentment, it is always a contentment with one's sensible condition. Watson acknowledges this by claiming that con-

tentment cannot be attained without attending to our natural needs and desires (83). So, the notion of happiness as contentment need not remove happiness from the sensible realm.

7. This use of *Zufriedenheit* to describe happiness does not make happiness a nonsensible state. Insofar as happiness is said to be contentment, it is, in all these passages, a contentment with one's physical state. So while this contentment is not equivalent to that physical state, this notion of contentment does not remove happiness from the realm of the sensible. In contrast, section II considers several passages that link happiness to a moral contentment [*Zufriedenheit*], a contentment with one's moral state. This notion of contentment would remove happiness from the realm of the sensible.

8. See, for instance, H. J. Paton, "Kant's Idea of the Good," *Proceedings of the Aristotelian Society* 45 (1944-45), ix, and *The Categorical Imperative* (Chicago: University of Chicago Press, 1948), 85, and *The Moral Law* (London: Hutchinson's, 1947), 29; Mary Gregor, *Laws of Freedom* (Oxford: B. Blackwell, 1963), 78; L. W. Beck, *A Commentary on Kant's Critique of Practical Reason* (Chicago: University of Chicago Press, 1960), 72, 98; Viggo Rossvaer, *Kant's Moral Philosophy*, 134; and Klaus Düsing, "Das Problem des höchsten Gutes in Kants praktischer Philosophie," *Kant-Studien* 62 (1971), 23-27.

9. My emphasis throughout.

10. My emphasis.

11. See A800/B828 where Kant speaks of uniting all the ends prescribed to us by our desires into one single end, happiness; and TP,49/8,282 where happiness is called "an end supplied by nature" and is identified as the attainment of the sum of all ends. Also, see R. Z. Friedman, "Virtue and Happiness: Kant and Three Critics," *Canadian Journal of Philosophy* 11:1 (1981), 95, who describes happiness as "the fulfillment of all of one's wants."

12. Kant describes happiness as both an Idea (Gr.67/4,399) and an Ideal (Gr.86/4,418). He defines an "idea" as "a necessary concept of reason to which no corresponding object can be given in sense-experience" (A327/B383) and the "ideal" as "the idea, . . . as an individual thing, determinable or

even determined by the idea alone" (A568/B596). Kant calls happiness an "Idea" in order to stress that while happiness is a totality, it is not a totality that corresponds to any sensible object. Kant is not here denying that happiness is sensible, that is, defined in terms of inclination. He is denying only that it can be given in its totality as a sensible object. Similarly, Kant seems to call happiness an Ideal of imagination in order to emphasize that happiness is thought as a singular totality and that it is not a rational, determinate totality (but an empirical totality, a totality of imagination).

13. See Paton who in "Kant's Idea of the Good," x, and in *The Categorical Imperative*, 86, finds other reasons to prefer the description of happiness as the realization of a system of inclinations to the description of happiness as the realization of all inclinations.

14. Other commentators have noted that there is some connection between happiness and pleasure. Among them are: Beck, *A Commentary on Kant's Critique of Practical Reason*, 98; Gregor, *Laws of Freedom*, 78; Paton, *The Moral Law*, 29; and Paul Schilpp, *Kant's Pre-Critical Ethics* (Evanston: Northwestern University Press, 1960), 42.

15. L. W. Beck calls this fragment "Duisburg Fragment 6," locates it in volume 19 of the Academy Edition, and dates it just after the first *Critique* (Beck, *A Commentary*, 215). Paul Schilpp finds the fragment in R. Reicke, *Lose Blätter aus Kants Nachlass* 1 (Königsberg: Beyer's, 1889), 9-16, and dates it in the middle of the 1770s (Schilpp, *Kant's Pre-Critical Ethics*, 127-30). In the passages quoted from the fragment, I use Schilpp's translations and give the page numbers from his book, followed by the corresponding volume and page numbers from the Academy Edition. In cases where Schilpp has no translation of a passage, I give my own translation and cite only the volume and page number from the Academy Edition.

16. Beck, *A Commentary*, 216.

17. Kant's use of the term "analogue" is interesting and brings to mind his claim in the first *Critique* that we can think a wise and omnipotent Author of the world by analogy with an empirical concept (A698/B726) and by analogy with realities in the world (A678/B706).

18. This explains why Kant is more critical of the attempt to define moral happiness as happiness than he is of the attempts to define self-contentment and bliss as happiness. "Moral happiness," as he says, is a self-contradiction and while neither self-contentment nor bliss amount to happiness either, at least the terms as such are not self-contradictory.

19. Watson, in "Kant on Happiness in the Moral Life," 91, says that self-contentment is "analogous to" bliss.

20. Happiness also includes the idea of an infinite although not the idea of infinite progress. See Gr.85-86 where Kant says happiness involves an infinite number of inclinations.

21. Among some of the states there are other similarities as well.

22. See chapter 6, section III for some further reflections on this connection.

Chapter 2

1. "*einen Willen, d.i. ein Vermögen haben, ihre Causalität durch die Vorstellung von Regeln zu bestimmen, mithin so fern sie der handlungen nach Grundsätzen, folglich auch nach praktischen Principien a priori.*"

2. "*so ist der Wille nichts anders als praktische Vernunft.*"

3. "*Vernunft . . . die Maxime des Willens bei einer handlung jederzeit an den reinen Willen halte, d.i. an sich selbst, indem sie sich als a priori praktisch betrachtet.*"

4. H. J. Paton, in "Kant's Idea of the Good," *Proceedings of the Aristotelian Society* 45 (1944-45), xv, says that an action is good in virtue of the principle in accordance with which it is willed and not in virtue of its matter or in virtue of what is willed.

5. See Allen Buchanan, "Categorical Imperatives and Moral Principles," *Philosophical Studies* 31 (1977), 256-59, who agrees that Kant wants to show that moral principles can be justified without the aid of empirical premisses. But, Buchanan argues, all that can be shown in fact is that the

ground of moral obligation is not empirical since some moral laws (e.g. the principle of beneficence) require empirical premisses.

6. Andrews Reath, "Hedonism, Heteronomy and Kant's Principle of Happiness," *Pacific Philosophical Quarterly* 70 (1989), 59, argues persuasively that the principle of happiness is not defined by its choice of any particular object but by the way in which it directs choice by assigning value to ends.

7. See Gary Watson, "Kant on Happiness in the Moral Life," *Philosophy Research Archives* 9 (1983), 98, who also notes that contrary to Kant's claim, not all material principles are subsumed under the principle of self-love; and Andrews Reath, "Hedonism, Heteronomy and Kant's Principle of Happiness," 63, who argues that the principle of happiness is neither hedonistic nor egoistic but is a general principle covering all material principles.

8. See Richard G. Henson, "What Kant Might Have Said: Moral Worth and the Overdetermination of Dutiful Action," *The Philosophical Review* 88 (1979), 42, who argues that while Kant seems to assume an act will be motivated either by duty or by inclination, in fact many acts have several motives (are "overdetermined").

9. See Thomas E. Hill, Jr., "The Hypothetical Imperative," *The Philosophical Review* 82 (1973), 443-44, who concludes that imperatives are hypothetical when information about the agent's ends (i.e., a certain type of empirical information) is necessary to apply or to rationally defend the prescription.

Chapter 3

1. John Atwell, in *Ends and Principles in Kant's Moral Thought* (Dordrecht: Nijhoff, 1986), 9, claims that when Kant distinguishes between subjective and objective ends, *Zweck* is always used for objective end while subjective end is *Zweck, Absicht, Gegenstand,* or *Objekt.* See section II below.

2. See, for instance, Rel.51 and Gr.73.

3. It is interesting to note that the end of pure reason is said to be humanity in the *Groundwork* while it is one's own

perfection and the happiness of others in the *Metaphysics of Morals*. I will not pursue this difference here since it is not germane to my task.

4. "*Zweck ist ein Gegenstand der Willkür (eines vernünftigen Wesens), durch dessen Vorstellung diese zu einer handlung diesen Gegenstand hervorzubringen bestimmt wird.*"

5. "*den Willen durch das Vermögen der Zwecke definiren konnte, indem sie jederzeit Bestimmungsgründe des Begehrungsvermögen nach Principien sind.*"

6. "*ein Zweck aber als Object, welches vor der Willensbestimmung durch eine praktische Regel vorhergehen und den Grund der Möglichkeit einer solchen enthalten muss, mithin die Materie des Willens, als Bestimmungsgrund desselben genommen, jederzeit empirisch ist.*"

7. "*Nun ist das, was dem Willen zum objectiven Grunde seiner Selbstbestimmung dient, der Zweck.*"

8. See H. J. Paton's translation of *Groundwork of the Metaphysic of Morals* (New York: Harper, 1964), 138n63, n. 2, where he comments on his decision to substitute "subjective" for "objective" in this passage. Andrews Reath, "Kant's Theory of Moral Sensibility," *Kant-Studien* 80 (1989), 285-87, considers respect for the moral law to be the direct though subjective determining ground of the will. By subjective he means "in the subject."

9. "*was als Zweck an sich selbst ein Grund bestimmter Gesetze sein könnte, so würde in ihm und nur in ihm allein der Grund eines möglichen kategorischen Imperativs, d.i. praktischen Gesetzes, liegen.*"

10. H. J. Paton, in *The Categorical Imperative* (Chicago: University of Chicago Press, 1948), 167-68, recognizes in Kant a tendency to identify ends with determining grounds of the will. He observes that Kant is looking for an absolute end which would ground categorical imperatives in the same way that relative ends ground hypothetical imperatives.

11. "*die moralische Zwecklehre, die von Pflichten handelt auf a priori in der reinen praktischen Vernunft gegebenen Principien beruht.*"

12. "*Die Materie eines praktischen Princips ist der Gegenstand des Willens. Dieser ist entweder der Bestimmungsgrund des letzteren oder nicht.*"

13. Roger J. Sullivan, *Immanuel Kant's Moral Theory* (Cambridge: Cambridge University Press, 1989), 64-65, seems to take the traditional approach when he argues that duties cannot be grounded on ends, even objective ends, since the result would be heteronomy. Yet, when he observes that Kant incorporates ends into morality without falling into heteronomy by grounding ends in the moral law, he makes possible the interpretation offered here of ends as secondary determining grounds.

14. See Richard G. Henson, "What Kant Might Have Said: Moral Worth and the Overdetermination of Dutiful Action," *The Philosophical Review* 88 (1979), 44-45, and Henning Jensen, "Kant on Overdetermination, Indirect Duties, and Moral Worth," *Proceedings: Sixth International Kant Congress* (Washington, D.C.: University Press of America, 1989), 162, who speak of "cooperating motives" which are nonmoral motives sufficient by themselves (in the absence of other motives) to lead one to do an act required by duty. The ends here considered as determining grounds of the will are secondary determining grounds, not sufficient by themselves, since they follow from the moral law itself.

15. Bruce Aune, in *Kant's Theory of Morals* (Princeton: Princeton University Press, 1979), 107, draws a distinction between primary and secondary determining grounds of the pure will. He identifies the moral law as the primary determining ground of the will and the highest good as the secondary determining ground of the will. His distinction parallels the point being made here though he focuses on the highest good as secondary determining ground while I am allowing that any object of pure reason might act as secondary determining ground.

16. Andrews Reath, "Kant's Theory of Moral Sensibility," 285, focuses on incentives as subjective (in the subject) determining grounds of the will. Hence, respect for the moral law is a subjective determining ground as is self-love (298). In the context of this work, subjective means concern for ends. Onora O'Neill, *Constructions of Reason* (Cambridge: Cambridge

University Press, 1989), 150, specifies two senses in which a principle is subjective: adopted by some agent at a particular time, and aimed at what that agent wants.

17. John E. Atwell, in *Ends and Principles in Kant's Moral Thought*, 95-96, is right when he states that objective ends should not be regarded as states of affairs so valuable that they, by themselves, generate duties to pursue them. He reaches this conclusion in a different way than I have by distinguishing between what objective ends are and what establishes them as objective ends.

18. Among those recognizing the positive value of happiness are Norman Kemp Smith, John Silber, and Paul Schilpp. Kemp Smith, in *A Commentary to Kant's Critique of Pure Reason* (New York: Humanities Press, 1962), 570-71, says: "Happiness has natural value." Silber, in "The Ethical Significance of Kant's *Religion*," part of the introduction to Greene and Hudson translation of Kant's *Religion Within the Limits of Reason Alone* (New York: Harper, 1960), cxiii n., argues that: "Kant's ethical position requires the existence of two basically different kinds of goodness-moral goodness and natural (*physische*) goodness." On page cxii n., Silber condemns those who fail to see "all of Kant's doctrines and texts which insist upon the goodness of happiness and express a concern for its fulfillment." Schilpp, in *Kant's Pre-critical Ethics* (Evanston: Northwestern University Press, 1960), 59, speaks of "Kant's admission of the ideal of happiness as one not to be despised." He claims on page 60 that Kant recognizes (in his *Observations on the Feelings of the Beautiful and the Sublime*) "that happiness is not only an actual and valid human desire, but also that ethics will have to take serious account of it."

Chapter 4

1. See H. J. Paton, "Kant's Idea of the Good," *Proceedings of the Aristotelian Society* 45 (1944-45), xx-xxi, and *The Categorical Imperative* (Chicago: University of Chicago Press, 1948), 57, 172; Sir David Ross, *Kant's Ethical Theory* (Westport: Greenwood Press, 1978; rpt. of Oxford: Clarendon Press, 1954), 16; John Silber, "The Ethical Significance of Kant's *Religion*," part of the introduction to Greene and Hudson translation of Kant's *Religion Within the Limits of*

Reason Alone (New York: Harper, 1960), cxiii n; John Atwell, *Ends and Principles in Kant's Moral Thought* (Dordrecht: Nijhoff, 1986), 119; Viggo Rossvaer, *Kant's Moral Philosophy* (Oslo: Universitetsforlaget, 1979), 52; and Henning Jensen, "Kant on Overdetermination, Indirect Duties, and Moral Worth," *Proceedings: Sixth International Kant Congress* (Washington, D.C.: University Press of America, 1989), 164.

2. I include here L. W. Beck, Patrick Hutchings, T. C. Williams, and Keith Ward. Bruce Aune, however, says something about the duty to pursue personal happiness although it seems to be the wrong thing. He states, in *Kant's Theory of Morals* (Princeton: Princeton University Press, 1979), 36, that "we have, Kant thinks, no actual obligation to pursue our own happiness." He claims later on pages 189, 190 that Kant's ethics does not specify the means or make it an ethical requirement to adopt certain means to obligatory ends. Yet, it seems that Kant has done just that. Either Aune fails to see Kant's discussion of a person's indirect duty to pursue personal happiness or else Aune means by "actual obligation" a direct duty and so he is commenting only on the lack of a direct duty to pursue personal happiness.

3. "*Seine eigene Glückseligkeit sichern, ist Pflicht (wenigstens indirect), denn der Mangel der Zufriedenheit mit seinem Zustande in einem Gedränge von vielen Sorgen und mitten unter unbefriedigten Bedürfnissen könnte leicht eine grosse Versuchung zu Ubertretung der Pflichten werden.*"

4. "*Es kann sogar in gewissem Betracht Pflicht sein, für seine Glückseligkeit zu sorgen: theils weil sie (wozu Geschicklichkeit, Gesundheit, Reichthum gehört) Mittel zu Erfüllung seiner Pflicht enthält, theils weil der Mangel derselben (z.B. Armuth) Versuchungen enthält, seine Pflicht zu übertreten. Nur, seine Glückseligkeit zu befördern, kann unmittelbar niemals Pflicht, noch weniger ein Princip aller Pflicht sein.*"

5. "*Wohlhabenheit für sich selbst zu suchen ist direct nicht Pflicht; aber indirect kann es eine solche wohl sein.*"

6. In section III, see Kant's talk of other means directed toward the same end.

7. Silber says: "The good will, therefore is itself the object of the will, and in its act of volition it wills nothing more or less

than its own perfection (free willing) as an end which is also a duty." John R. Silber, "The Importance of the Highest Good in Kant's Ethics," *Ethics* 73 (1963), 186.

8. Roger J. Sullivan, in *Immanuel Kant's Moral Theory* (Cambridge: Cambridge University Press, 1989), 203, considers these four ways in which the duty to pursue personal happiness may arise: certain natural qualities make easier the task of the good will, certain comforts allow us to more easily attend to our moral duties, we may deserve happiness but lack it, and the principle of self-love may fail to motivate us to take care of ourselves.

9. I return to these other indirect duties in section III.

10. Some of Paton's claims reflect this same difference. He refers, in *The Categorical Imperative*, 57, to "the everyday happiness which every man has a right, and even an indirect duty, to seek in his own way, so long as this is not incompatible with duty." He later states on page 172 that: "It may, however, be our duty to seek our own happiness as a means to our moral welfare." The first statement claims that it is a person's indirect duty to seek personal happiness, while the second says it may be a duty to seek happiness. However, one problem with Paton's claims is that the first statement suggests that it is possible while acting out of an indirect duty to seek happiness that one might act in a way incompatible with duty. But Kant has labeled this former duty "indirect" to show that it is a duty only in its role as a means to morality. As such, the seeking of happiness cannot be incompatible with duty; it is a means to the performance of duty. Perhaps Paton was treating happiness as an end in itself, in which case, the pursuit of happiness can conflict with duty since then the action is done for the sake of happiness and not for the sake of morality.

11. This distinction between the pursuit of a thing and the possession of a thing is noted by John R. Silber in his study of the highest good. He states that: "Our duty as defined by the moral law is not to attain but to promote with all our strength the highest good as the object and final end of pure practical reason." See Silber, "Kant's Conception of the Highest Good as Immanent and Transcendent," *The Philosophical Review* 68 (1959), 478.

12. Though, as a matter of fact, in this section of the second *Critique*, Kant denies there is a duty to pursue happiness. "A command that everyone should seek to make himself happy would be foolish, for no one commands another to do what he already invariably wishes to do" (CPR,38/5,37). Kant is, I believe, denying that there is a duty to pursue happiness as an *end*, which does not however mean that there is no duty to pursue happiness as a *means* to morality.

13. See below a discussion of Kant's ambiguity in treating *andere Wesen.*

14. "*Diese zielen auch indirekt auf die Pflichten der Menschheit ab.*"

15. "*Allein weil Tiere nur als Mittel da sind, indem sie sich ihrer selbst nicht bewusst sind, der Mensch aber der Zweck ist . . . so haben wir gegen die Tiere unmittelbar keine Pflichten, sondern die Pflichten gegen die Tiere sind indirekte Pflichten gegen die Menschheit.*"

16. "*seine Pflicht in Ansehung anderer Wesen für Pflicht gegen diese Wesen.*"

17. "*nämlich in Ansehung dieser Thiere, direct aber betrachtet ist sie immer nur Pflicht des Menschen gegen sich selbst.*"

18. "*hat der Mensch sonst keine Pflicht, als blos gegen den Menschen.*"

Chapter 5

1. Donald Walhout, "Kant's Conception of Nonmoral Good," *Southwestern Journal of Philosophy* 3 (1972), 7, maintains that Kant's highest good is better rendered through Aristotle's notion of human fulfillment than through the notion which is in fact offered, virtue and happiness. He claims that the good is singular and that there is no reason why the achievement of virtue should not be considered part of a human being's happiness (11-12).

2. My translation from the German.

3. "*auf das höchste in der Welt mögliche Gut (die im Weltganzen mit der reinsten Sittlichkeit auch verbundene allgemeine, jener gemässe Glückseligkeit.*"

4. "*(die jener ihrer Beobachtung angemessne Glückseligkeit) zusammen vereinigt in sich enthält, das ist, die Idee eines höchsten Guts in der Welt.*"

5. "*Dieser Wille darf also zwar nicht das einzige und das ganze, aber er muss doch das höchste Gut und zu allem Ubrigen . . . sein.*"

6. "*das oberste Gut (als die erste Bedingung des höchsten Guts) Sittlichkeit . . . sei.*"

7. It is interesting to note that both the *Groundwork* and the second *Critique* deny that the good will, virtue, is *das ganze gut*, translated as "the complete good" and "the entire good." Virtue and happiness together is *das Ganze, das vollendete Gute*, said to be "the whole, the perfect good." Thus, the supreme good is defined in part by what it fails to be; namely, *das Ganze*, the complete, entire, whole good.

8. "*Woher haben wir aber den Begriff von Gott als dem höchsten Gut?*"

9. "*Die vollkommenste Welt ist das höchste erschaffene Gut.*"

10. "*das höchste in der Welt mögliche und, so viel an uns ist, als Endzweck zu befordernde physische Gut.*"

11. "*Folglich ist das Postulat der Möglichkeit des höchsten abgeleiteten Guts (der besten Welt) zugleich das Postulat der Wirklichkeit eines höchsten ursprünglichen Guts, nämlich der Existenz Gottes.*"

12. "*das abgeleitete höchste Gut möglich macht.*"

13. "*der heiligkeit seines Willens als dem höchsten ursprünglichen Gute.*"

14. "*des höchsten selbstständigen Guts, d.i. des Daseins Gottes.*"

15. John R. Silber and Thomas Auxter propose other definitions of the highest good. Silber, in "The Importance of the Highest Good in Kant's Ethics," *Ethics* 73 (1963), 193, claims that the highest good is the uniting of the "ends of perfection and happiness of others." There are passages in which one's own perfection and the happiness of others are identified as ends which are at the same time duties (MM,43/6,385-86).

But the happiness component in the highest good is certainly not restricted to the happiness of others. For example: "my own happiness is included in the concept of the highest good" (CPR,134/5,129). Auxter, in "The Unimportance of Kant's Highest Good," *Journal of the History of Philosophy* 17:2 (1979), 127, maintains that the highest good can mean either the "ectypal world" or happiness in proportion to worth. He claims that these two definitions show that the highest good means both a good to be achieved in this world and an other-worldly condition. Auxter is correct that there is ambiguity regarding the location of the highest good (see chapter 6). But it is not clear that Auxter is correct in suggesting that the highest good as ectypal world is something other than the highest good as happiness in proportion to worth (see CPR,44/5,43). Andrews Reath, in "Two Conceptions of the Highest Good in Kant," *Journal of the History of Philosophy* 26:4 (1988), 601, seems to make the same point as Auxter by distinguishing between a secular and a theological conception of the highest good. However, questions about the role or the location of the highest good do not, I believe, warrant separate definitions of the highest good or multiple highest goods.

16. Andrews Reath makes the same claim (Reath, "Two Conceptions of the Highest Good in Kant," 593). He goes on to describe the highest good in ways similar to those which follow. For instance, he speaks of the highest good as unconditioned object (597), as end (604n), as final end (594), and of the moral law which defines the final end as "not just a law for individual conduct, but . . . the basis of a social order" (617). Also, Steven G. Smith proposes four "rationalizations," reasons, for the highest good: motivation, unity of reason, content of moral will, and justice. See Smith, "Worthiness to be Happy and Kant's Concept of the Highest Good," *Kant-Studien* 75 (1984), 168-90. The first three will be considered in section III; the last is considered here in section II. Klaus Düsing, in "Das Problem des höchsten Gutes in Kants praktischer Philosophie," *Kant-Studien* 62 (1971), 5-42, claims that Kant assigns two functions to the highest good. In the *Critique of Practical Reason*, the highest good is the Kingdom of God. It is ideal, purely intellectual, but in the *Critique of Pure Reason* and in the *Reflexions* the highest good becomes an a priori principle, which makes possible the execution of the moral

law (16-20). Smith concludes that the variety in the descriptions of the highest good is due to the heterogeneity of virtue and happiness (184). Reath proposes that the reason for the different roles of the highest good is that Kant wanted to emphasize human agency and still keep to Leibniz's notion of the City of God (608-09n). On my view, at least as much of the blame for unclarity in the concept of the highest good is due to unclarity in Kant's definition of happiness. See section III of chapter 6.

17. John R. Silber seems to acknowledge this task of the highest good in claims from his article, "Procedural Formalism in Kant's Ethics," *The Review of Metaphysics* 28 (1974), 197-236. He states that the highest good is "the material *object* of volition" (198; emphasis mine) and that the attainment of the highest good is "the *goal* of the moral person" (200; emphasis mine).

18. For other examples, see: CPR,126/5,122; CPR,129/5,124; CPR,138/5,133; and CPR,139/5,134.

19. Three who have identified this role of the highest good are Norman Kemp Smith, *A Commentary to Kant's Critique of Pure Reason* (New York: Humanities Press, 1962), Allen W. Wood, *Kant's Moral Religion* (Ithaca: Cornell University Press, 1970), and Terry F. Godlove, "Moral Actions, Moral Lives: Kant on Intending the Highest Good," *The Southern Journal of Philosophy* 25:1 (1987), 49-64. Kemp Smith says: "Reason . . . prescribes, as the final and complete end of all our actions . . . happiness proportioned to moral worth" (574). Wood and Godlove note that the highest good is the final end and contrast it with particular, immediate ends (Wood, 98-99; Godlove, 55). Wood concludes that not pursuing the highest good makes impossible moral volition itself and thus the pursuit of particular ends (158) while Godlove asserts that nontheists do pursue particular ends though they cannot pursue the final end (55). What follows shows that the final end is simply the entirety of all ends and it is at least logically possible for a person to will a single end without willing all ends. The disagreement between Wood and Godlove really raises the question of the importance of the highest good. See section III.

20. Given the number of passages which state that the highest good is an end of the will, indeed the final end of the

will, it is hard to be persuaded by R. Z. Friedman's assertion that the highest good is *not* an end of moral experience. He argues in his article, "Hypocrisy and the Highest Good: Hegel on Kant's Transition from Morality to Religion," *Journal of the History of Philosophy* 24:4 (1986), 503-22, that "the highest good, is likewise, I believe, a condition of the possibility of moral experience, not an end of moral experience" (508). Possibly Kant *should* have said it is a condition of the possibility of moral experience, but he *says* it is an end of the will, of pure practical reason.

21. Reath, in "Two Conceptions of the Highest Good in Kant," 597, says as final end, the highest good "should be interpreted as the totality or the complete set of ends that could result from moral conduct."

22. Two who have recognized that the highest good can be proposed as an individual end or as a social end are John R. Silber, "The Importance of the Highest Good in Kant's Ethics," and Steven G. Smith, "Worthiness to be Happy and Kant's Concept of the Highest Good." Silber speaks of the highest good for an individual, the attaining of personal happiness in proportion to a person's virtue, and the highest good possible in the world, the attaining of happiness in proportion to worth in the lives of all people (194-95). Smith claims that one of the "rationalizations" for the highest good is its embodiment as a principle of justice. The highest good as a principle of justice can be manifested on three levels: individual, social, and divine (179). Both of the latter two would fall under my consideration of the highest good as social end since I am interested only in establishing that the highest good can be a personal goal or a worldwide goal. I am not now concerned with *where* this social end might be realized or *by whom*.

23. My translation.

24. See chapter 6.

25. See John R. Silber, "Kant's Conception of the Highest Good as Immanent and Transcendent," *The Philosophical Review* 68 (1959), 469-92, "The Importance of the Highest Good in Kant's Ethics," 179-97, "Procedural Formalism in Kant's Ethics," 197-236; Mary-Barbara Zeldin, "The Summum Bonum, the Moral Law, and the Existence of God," *Kant-Studien* 62 (1971), 43-54; Gerald W. Barnes, "In Defense of

Kant's Doctrine of the Highest Good," *Philosophical Forum* 2 (1971), 446-58; R. Z. Friedman, "The Importance and Function of Kant's Highest Good," *Journal of the History of Philosophy* 22:3 (1984), 325-42.

26. See L. W. Beck, *A Commentary on Kant's Critique of Practical Reason* (Chicago: University of Chicago Press, 1960); Thomas Auxter, "The Unimportance of Kant's Highest Good," 121-34; Jeffrie Murphy, "The Highest Good as Content of Kant's Ethical Formalism," *Kant-Studien* 56 (1965), 102-10.

27. This is a point Mary-Barbara Zeldin makes in her article, "The Summum Bonum, the Moral Law, and the Existence of God." On page 50, she says: "Heteronomy is not, however, involved . . . since the *summum bonum* as the goal is not the determining factor." I however go on to argue that the highest good is the determining ground of the will although there is still no heteronomy involved.

28. Silber, "Procedural Formalism in Kant's Ethics," 198.

29. Zeldin, "The Summum Bonum, the Moral Law, and the Existence of God," 48.

30. Murphy, "The Highest Good as Content of Kant's Ethical Formalism," 102.

31. Ibid., 105.

32. Ibid., 106.

33. See Beck, *A Commentary on Kant's Critique of Practical Reason*, 245, and Friedman, "The Importance and Function of Kant's Highest Good," 326.

34. Beck, *A Commentary on Kant's Critique of Practical Reason*, 243.

35. Friedman, "The Importance and Function of Kant's Highest Good," 327.

36. Andrews Reath, "Two Conceptions of the Highest Good in Kant," echoes this interpretation of the highest good though he does not link it to the question of the determining grounds of the will. He claims that the highest good is "an end to be constructed out of the Moral Law" (599). Bruce Aune, *Kant's Theory of Morals* (Princeton: Princeton University Press, 1979), identifies the highest good as a determining ground of the will. Aune says

that "a rational being necessarily intends to do what he can to realize the highest good, but he does so *only because* he necessarily intends to conform to the universal laws he has freely made" (107). So Aune calls the moral law the primary determining ground of the will and the highest good the secondary determining ground of the will. See the discussion in chapter 3, section II concerning ends as determining grounds of the will.

37. Beck, *A Commentary on Kant's Critique of Practical Reason*, 245.

38. Ibid., 244-45.

39. Murphy, "The Highest Good as Content for Kant's Ethical Formalism," 107.

40. See also Silber, "Procedural Formalism in Kant's Ethics," 235, who speaks of the "duty to promote the embodiment of the highest good," and Zeldin, "The Summum Bonum, the Moral Law, and the Existence of God," 49, who argues that "the command to promote the *summum bonum* . . . is found in the third formulation of the categorical imperative."

41. See, for example, L. W. Beck, *A Commentary on Kant's Critique of Practical Reason*, 243, who claims the concept of the highest good is not necessary to the definition of duty; R. Z. Friedman, "The Importance and Function of Kant's Highest Good," 331, who states "the highest good commands no more than does the moral law;" and T. Auxter, "The Unimportance of Kant's Highest Good," 122, who argues "the case against using the highest good as a moral standard."

42. See, for example, Silber, "Kant's Conception of the Highest Good as Immanent and Transcendent," 484-85, where he claims that the idea of the highest good as an object to be promoted by man "is the measure which specifies man's actual moral obligation." Zeldin, "The Summum Bonum, the Moral Law, and the Existence of God," 49-50, claims that the concept of the *summum bonum* contains more than the concept of morality. She concludes that the *summum bonum* is not analytically connected with morality but is synthetically a priori connected with it (53).

43. Rel.5/6,5 says that harmony with the concept of a final end does not add to a person's duties, though TP,46/8,279 says it is "another" end [*einen andern Zweck*].

44. See Allen W. Wood, *Kant's Moral Religion*, 98-99, 158, and Terry F. Godlove, "Moral Actions, Moral Lives: Kant on Intending the Highest Good," 50, 55; both of whom argue that the highest good is the end of a moral life and not the end of this or that action.

45. This point has been made by Gerald W. Barnes, "In Defense of Kant's Doctrine of the Highest Good," 453-54, and Sharon Anderson-Gold, "Kant's Ethical Commonwealth: The Highest Good as a Social Goal," *International Philosophical Quarterly* 26:1 (1986), 30. Barnes says that the duty to keep promises and the duty to be virtuous are duties of individuals while the duty to bring about the highest good and the duty to be happy are collective duties, not duties of individuals. Anderson-Gold however goes on to say that people have an obligation to contribute what they can to promote a social union since an individual's good and virtue is only achieved in a social community (30-31). She seems to speak of the duty to further the highest good as both a collective and an individual duty.

46. See, for instance, Murphy, "The Highest Good as Content for Kant's Ethical Formalism," 102, who says the highest good is an unnecessary notion.

47. Beck states that: "the concept of the highest good is not a practical concept at all . . . It is not important in Kant's philosophy for any practical consequences it might have, for it has none except those drawn from the concept of *bonum supremum*," *A Commentary on Kant's Critique of Practical Reason*, 245.

48. See Silber, "The Importance of the Highest Good in Kant's Ethics," 195. Zeldin too maintains that the highest good is an important concept and necessary to morality ("The Summum Bonum, the Moral Law, and the Existence of God," 53).

49. This is perhaps what Friedman means when he says the highest good is an important practical concept but only because it is a condition for the possibility of the moral law. See Friedman, "The Importance and Function of Kant's Highest Good," 326-27, and "Hypocrisy and the Highest Good: Hegel on Kant's Transition from Morality to Religion," 508.

Chapter 6

1. This is my translation since Kemp Smith uses "supreme good."

2. On the following pages there is at least one and often several references to "*das höchste Gut*," translated by Beck as "the highest good." Here I list first the page number from Beck's translation and second the corresponding page from volume 5 of the Academy edition. See CPR,4/4, 112/108, 113/109, 114/109, 115/111, 116/112, 117/113, 118/114, 119/115, 123/119, 124/119, 126/122, 127/122, 127/123, 128/124, 129/125, 130/126, 131/126, 133/128, 134/129, 134/130, 135/130, 135/131, 137/132, 138/133, 139/134, 140/135, 141/136, 143/138, 144/139, 145/140, 148/142, 148/143, 149/144, 150/145, 151/145, 151/146, and 153/147.

3. "*nur ein Ideal, das ist: ein Muster, Idee, ein Urbild aller unserer Begriffe vom Guten.*"

4. I use my own translations here since the Infield translation uses "supreme" where Kant says "*höchste.*" See what follows on pages 153-55.

5. "*Das höchste in der Welt mögliche und, so viel an uns ist, als Endzweck zu befordernde physische Gut ist Glückseligkeit: unter der objectiven Bedingung der Einstimmung des Menschen mit dem Gesetze der Sittlichkeit, als der Würdigkeit glücklich zu sein.*"

6. "*einer mit der Befolgung moralischer Gesetze harmonisch zusammentreffender Glückseligkeit vernünftiger Wesen, als den höchsten Weltbesten.*"

7. "*Wir sind a priori durch die Vernunft bestimmt, des Weltbeste, . . . nach allen Kräften zu befordern.*"

8. "*Dergleichen ist das höchste durch Freiheit zu bewirkende Gut in der Welt.*"

9. See my earlier discussion of this definition of the highest good in chapter 5, section I.

10. Wolfgang Schwarz's translation of Kant's *Critique of Pure Reason* (Darmstadt: Scientia Verlag Aalen, 1982), 245, 247, does not make this error as he translates "*höchste*" as "highest," not "supreme."

11. See, for instance, John R. Silber, "Kant's Conception of the Highest Good as Immanent and Transcendent," *The Philosophical Review* 68 (1959), 484-86; Thomas Auxter, "The Unimportance of Kant's Highest Good," *Journal of the History of Philosophy* 17:2 (1979), 127; Steven G. Smith, "Worthiness to be Happy and Kant's Concept of the Highest Good," *Kant-Studien* 75 (1984), 173; and Andrews Reath, "Two Conceptions of the Highest Good in Kant," *Journal of the History of Philosophy* 26:4 (1988), 601.

12. See, for instance, Thomas Auxter, "The Unimportance of Kant's Highest Good," 127; and Andrews Reath, "Two Conceptions of the Highest Good in Kant," 600-01.

13. John R. Silber, "The Importance of the Highest Good in Kant's Ethics," *Ethics* 73 (1963), 184-85.

14. See CPR,124-26/5,119-21.

Bibliography

Anderson-Gold, Sharon. "Kant's Ethical Commonwealth: The Highest Good as a Social Goal," *International Philosophical Quarterly* 26:1 (1986) 23-32.

Atwell, John E. *Ends and Principles in Kant's Moral Thought* (Dordrecht: Nijhoff, 1986).

Aune, Bruce. *Kant's Theory of Morals* (Princeton: Princeton University Press, 1979).

Auxter, Thomas. *Kant's Moral Teleology* (Macon: Mercer University Press, 1982).

———. "The Unimportance of Kant's Highest Good," *Journal of the History of Philosophy* 17:2 (1979) 121-34.

Barnes, Gerald W. "In Defense of Kant's Doctrine of the Highest Good," *Philosophical Forum* 2 (1971) 446-58.

Beck, Lewis White. *A Commentary on Kant's Critique of Practical Reason* (Chicago: University of Chicago Press, 1960).

Buchanan, Allen. "Categorical Imperatives and Moral Principles," *Philosophical Studies* 31 (1977) 249-60.

Düsing, Klaus. "Das Problem des höchsten Gutes in Kants praktischer Philosophie," *Kant-Studien* 62 (1971) 5-42.

Eggerman, Richard W. "Kant and Rational Imperatives of Happiness," *Southwestern Journal of Philosophy* 11 (1980) 43-50.

Fischer, Norbert. "Tugend und Glückseligkeit: Zu ihrem Verhältnis bei Aristoteles und Kant," *Kant-Studien* 74 (1983) 1-21.

Friedman, R. Z. "Hypocrisy and the Highest Good: Hegel on Kant's Transition from Morality to Religion," *Journal of the History of Philosophy* 24:4 (1986) 503-22.

———. "The Importance and Function of Kant's Highest Good," *Journal of the History of Philosophy* 22:3 (1984) 325-42.

———. "Virtue and Happiness: Kant and Three Critics," *Canadian Journal of Philosophy* 11:1 (1981) 95-110.

Godlove, Terry F. "Moral Actions, Moral Lives: Kant on Intending the Highest Good," *The Southern Journal of Philosophy* 25:1 (1987) 49-64.

Greene, Theodore M. "The Historical Context and Religious Significance of Kant's *Religion*," part of the introduction to Greene and Hudson translation of Kant's *Religion Within the Limits of Reason Alone* (New York: Harper, 1960) ix-xxvii.

Gregor, Mary J. *Laws of Freedom* (Oxford: B. Blackwell, 1963).

Henson, Richard G. "What Kant Might Have Said: Moral Worth and the Overdetermination of Dutiful Action," *The Philosophical Review* 88 (1979) 39-54.

Hill Jr., Thomas E. "The Hypothetical Imperative," *The Philosophical Review* 82 (1973) 429-50.

Hutchings, Patrick. *Kant on Absolute Value* (Detroit: Wayne State University Press, 1972).

Jensen, Henning. "Kant on Overdetermination, Indirect Duties, and Moral Worth," *Proceedings: Sixth International Kant Congress* (Washington, D.C.: University Press of America, 1989) 161-70.

Keyworth, Donald R. "Kant's Concept of Happiness in the Moral Argument," *Personalist* 43 (1962) 21-33.

McGill, V. J. *The Idea of Happiness* (New York: Praeger, 1967).

Murphy, Jeffrie. "The Highest Good as Content of Kant's Ethical Formalism," *Kant-Studien* 56 (1965) 102-10.

O'Connor, Daniel. "Kant's Conception of Happiness," *The Journal of Value Inquiry* 16 (1982) 189-205.

O'Neill, Onora. *Constructions of Reason* (Cambridge: Cambridge University Press, 1989).

Paton, H. J. *The Categorical Imperative* (Chicago:University of Chicago Press, 1948).

———. *The Moral Law* (London: Hutchinson's, 1947).

———. "Kant's Idea of the Good," *Proceedings of the Aristotelian Society* 45 (1944-45) ii-xxv.

Reath, Andrews. "Kant's Theory of Moral Sensibility," *Kant-Studien* 80 (1989) 284-303.

———. "Hedonism, Heteronomy and Kant's Principle of Happiness," *Pacific Philosophical Quarterly* 70 (1989) 42-72.

———. "Two Conceptions of the Highest Good in Kant," *Journal of the History of Philosophy* 26:4 (1988) 593-620.

Ross, Sir David. *Kant's Ethical Theory* (Westport: Greenwood Press, 1978; rpt. of Oxford: Clarendon Press, 1954).

Rossvaer, Viggo. *Kant's Moral Philosophy* (Oslo: Universitetsforlaget, 1979).

Schilpp, P. A. *Kant's Pre-critical Ethics* (Evanston: Northwestern University Press, 1960).

Schroeder, H. H. "Some Common Misinterpretations of the Kantian Ethics," *The Philosophical Review* 49 (1940) 424-46.

Silber, John R. "Procedural Formalism in Kant's Ethics," *The Review of Metaphysics* 28 (1974) 197-236.

———. "The Importance of the Highest Good in Kant's Ethics," *Ethics* 73 (1963) 179-97.

———. "The Ethical Significance of Kant's *Religion*," part of the introduction to Greene and Hudson translation of Kant's *Religion Within the Limits of Reason Alone* (New York: Harper, 1960) xxix-cxxxiv.

———. "Kant's Conception of the Highest Good as Immanent and Transcendent," *The Philosophical Review* 68 (1959) 469-92.

Singer, Marcus G. *Generalization in Ethics* (London: Eyre & Spottiswoode Ltd., 1963).

Smith, Norman Kemp. *A Commentary to Kant's Critique of Pure Reason* (New York: Humanities Press, 1962).

Smith, Steven G. "Worthiness to be Happy and Kant's Concept of the Highest Good," *Kant-Studien* 75 (1984) 168-90.

Sullivan, Roger J. *Immanuel Kant's Moral Theory* (Cambridge: Cambridge University Press, 1989).

Walhout, Donald. "Kant's Conception of Nonmoral Good," *Southwestern Journal of Philosophy* 3 (1972) 7-19.

Ward, Keith. *The Development of Kant's View of Ethics* (Oxford: B. Blackwell, 1972).

Watson, Gary. "Kant on Happiness in the Moral Life," *Philosophy Research Archives* 9 (1983) 79-108.

Wike, Victoria S. "Does Kant's ethics require that the moral law be the sole determining ground of the will?," *The Journal of Value Inquiry* 27 (1993) 85-92.

———. "Kant on the Indirect Duty to Pursue Personal Happiness," *Akten des 7. Internationalen Kant-Kongresses* (Bonn: Bouvier Verlag, 1991) 599-611.

———. "Kant on Happiness," *Philosophy Research Archives* 13 (1988) 79-90.

———. "The Role of Happiness in Kant's *Groundwork*," *The Journal of Value Inquiry* 21 (1987) 73-79.

Williams, T. C. *The Concept of the Categorical Imperative* (Oxford: Clarendon, 1968).

Wood, Allen W. *Kant's Moral Religion* (Ithaca: Cornell University Press, 1970).

Zeldin, Mary-Barbara. "The Summum Bonum, the Moral Law, and the Existence of God," *Kant-Studien* 62 (1971) 43-54.

Index